REVISION
WORKS

FOR **JUNIOR** CERTIFICATE

ENGLISH

REVISION WORKS

FOR **JUNIOR** CERTIFICATE

ENGLISH

HIGHER LEVEL

Aoife O'Driscoll

educate.ie

PUBLISHED BY:
Educate.ie
Walsh Educational Books Ltd
Castleisland, Co. Kerry, Ireland
www.educate.ie

EDITOR:
Adam Brophy

PRODUCTION EDITOR:
Kieran O'Donoghue

DESIGN:
The Design Gang, Tralee

PRINTED AND BOUND BY:
Walsh Colour Print, Castleisland

ISBN: 978-1-908507-39-6

Acknowledgements

I would like to thank everyone at Educate.ie for their help and support, particularly Adam Brophy for his wonderfully constructive advice, patience and encouragement during the writing process. I would also like to thank Janette Condon for her practical and helpful suggestions; Peter Malone for overseeing the work; and the design team for creating such a visually pleasing book.

Dedication

This book is dedicated to my husband Tim and to my children Conor, Niamh and Killian.

Aoife O'Driscoll

CONTENTS

1 Finding Your Bearings — 8

2 Reading — 26

3 Personal Writing — 44

4 Functional Writing — 60

5 Media Studies — 114

6 Unseen Drama — 138

7 Studied Drama — 158

8 Unseen Poetry — 174

9 Studied Poetry — 190

10 Unseen Fiction — 232

11 Studied Fiction — 242

FINDING YOUR BEARINGS

There are two papers in the Junior Certificate English Exam. Both papers are allotted equal marks.

Paper 1: 180 marks

Paper 2: 180 marks

Total for Paper 1 and Paper 2: 360 marks

PAPER 1

Paper 1 is the **language** paper and it is divided into four sections.

Reading: 40 marks

Personal Writing: 70 marks

Functional Writing: 30 marks

Media Studies: 40 marks

The time allowed for Paper 1 is two and a half hours.

PAPER 2

Paper 2 is the **literature** paper and it is divided into three sections: drama, poetry and fiction. Each section is worth 60 marks.

Section 1: Drama

Unseen Drama: 30 marks

Studied Drama: 30 marks

Section 2: Poetry

Unseen Poetry: 30 marks

Studied Poetry: 30 marks

Section 3: Fiction

Unseen Fiction: 30 marks

Studied Fiction: 30 marks

The time allowed for Paper 2 is two and a half hours.

Recap

Paper 1: Language – 180 marks – two and a half hours

Paper 2: Literature – 180 marks – two and a half hours

COMMONLY ASKED QUESTIONS

Q Why is it important to know the breakdown of the marks for each paper?

A Students often ignore certain aspects of the course when they are revising, their reasoning being that the Studied Drama and Studied Poetry sections of Paper 2 are the most important parts of the Junior Cert English examination. However, it is worth noting that the marks for Functional Writing, for example, are exactly the same as the marks for each section of Paper 2. In other words, a detailed knowledge of *Romeo and Juliet* (or whichever play you have studied) is no more or less important than your ability to write a formal letter or a set of instructions. If you want to get a high grade in the exam, you should ensure that you revise for each and every section of Paper 1 and Paper 2.

Another reason to know how many marks are allotted to each question is that the amount of time you spend on a question should be determined by how many marks that question is worth.

Q How long should I spend on each question?

A Proper exam timing is vital if you want to get a high grade. If, for example, you over-run each of the first five answers on Paper 2 by five minutes, you will have no time to answer the sixth question. Here is a breakdown of the length of time you should spend on each question in Paper 1 and Paper 2.

Paper 1

Reading: 35 minutes   Personal Writing: 55 minutes

Functional Writing: 25 minutes   Media Studies: 35 minutes

Paper 2

Drama: 50 minutes (25 minutes each for Unseen and Studied)

Poetry: 50 minutes (25 minutes each for Unseen and Studied)

Fiction: 50 minutes (25 minutes each for Unseen and Studied)

Q How will I make sure I don't run out of time on the day of the exam?

A The best way to ensure that you don't run out of time is to practise answering questions under exam conditions from January or February on. Work through the past papers and force yourself to stick to the time limits given above. If your teacher sets past exam questions as homework assignments, you have an ideal opportunity to practise your timing. Of course, you should always do your best when doing your homework, and you should not rush it, but it is a good idea to write a rough draft of an answer first, and then to revise and rewrite it before handing it up to your teacher.

Buy a watch and watch your time

On the day of the exam take your watch off and put it on the desk in front of you. If you don't have a watch, get one between now

and the Junior Cert as phones will not be allowed into the exam hall. Keep checking that you are within the time you have allowed yourself for the question and, if you are running out of time, wind up your answer quickly and leave a space beneath it if necessary. You can always come back to it if you have a few minutes to spare at the end of the exam.

Q Do I have to answer the questions in the order in which they appear on the exam paper?

A No. You can answer the questions in any order you like. However, there is a difference between Paper 1 and Paper 2 when it comes to the order in which you should answer the questions, in that some of the tasks on Paper 1 can be based on earlier sections.

For example, in 2009 one of the Functional Writing tasks asked the following:

> *In Section One of this examination paper Michael Morpugo writes about the elements that he considers important to produce a piece of writing. Write a letter to the author in which you recount a time when you feel you wrote particularly well and explain what you think contributed to the success. In your letter you may, if you wish, comment on the earlier passage by Morpugo or seek his advice as a writer.*

Obviously, it would be far easier for you to write this letter if you had already answered the questions in Section 1 (Reading).

Paper 2 is different. The questions are not based on anything that may have appeared in earlier sections but always stand alone. In this paper, you can answer the questions in any order you wish, without running the risk of wasting valuable time.

It's always a good idea to start with the question you find easiest. If fiction is your favourite part of Paper 2, you may wish to start with that section. Remember to number all your questions very carefully. Do not assume the examiner will know which question you are answering.

Q If I have the time, should I answer an extra question or two?

A It is not advisable to answer any extra questions. You will need all the time allowed to plan and write your answers properly. If you do have any extra time left over at the end of the exam, recheck your answers and correct any mistakes you find.

Q Do I have to tell the truth when writing a personal essay?

A You do not have to tell the truth when writing a personal essay. However, it is worth bearing in mind that you are more likely to write a coherent, believable, interesting essay if it is based on the truth. This topic is covered in more detail in the Personal Writing section of this book (Chapter 3).

Q Can I use bad language, text language, slang and/or symbols in my writing?

A It is not a good idea to use bad language, text language or symbols in your writing. The only occasions where such language may be acceptable are when you are quoting from a set text or when you are using dialogue in a short story or personal essay. Even so, you should keep it to an absolute minimum.

EXAM TIPS

Read the questions carefully. **Paraphrase** them (put them in your own words) to see if you fully understand each one. Imagine you have to **explain** this question to someone who doesn't understand it. How would you break it down for them? **Underline** the key words in the question. Ask yourself how many parts there are to the question and how many marks each part carries. As a very general rule, if there are **ten marks** given for the question, you should aim to make **two or three points**.

Look out for the word 'and' in the question. If it is there, it may mean that there are two parts to the question. All too often, students do not achieve a high grade in the Junior Certificate English exam

because they do not read the question carefully enough, and only answer half of it. **You must ensure that your answer is balanced and that it deals with every part of the question**.

Know the marks – know the timing

The examiners are instructed to reward you for making several well-supported short points or fewer, more fully developed points. In general, it is better to make a few well-developed, well-supported points than to try to put down every piece of information you know. As a general rule, five marks equals one well-developed point. You should **make your point, explain it and back it up with suitable quotation or reference. Each point should be given a separate paragraph**.

Avoid simply giving a summary of the text. It doesn't matter how long your answer is, or how beautifully phrased it is: if you don't give your own analysis and make valid points which answer the question asked, you will not get a passing grade. Jot down a quick plan for your answer. This may be as simple as one or two words for each point you intend to make. If you do this, you will be less likely to repeat yourself, write a disorganised answer or forget what you wanted to say.

Look through each of the points you plan to make. Can each one be directly linked back to the question you have been asked? It is very easy to wander off the point; if you check this at the planning stage, it won't take you long to correct it.

When you are happy with your plan and have decided on the order in which you are going to write your points, begin your answer.

Make a point, develop it and support it with a suitable quotation or reference. Don't leave your quotations or references hanging in the middle of the answer: explain them by linking them to the point you are making. 'From this quote, we can see that ...' or 'We can see from the description of his facial expression that the character is angry: "John glowered menacingly at the small boy."'

Using a dictionary or thesaurus wil improve your vocabulary

Let the quotes speak for themselves when possible. Do not paraphrase a quote and then give the quote in its entirety. Here is a bad example of how to use a quote:

> *Yeats says that whenever he is standing on the road or on the grey pavements, he hears the Lake Isle of Innisfree deep in his heart: 'While I stand on the roadway, or on the pavements grey,/I hear it in the deep heart's core.'*

Here is a better way to incorporate the quote into the sentence:

> *Yeats' longing for the Lake Isle of Innisfree never leaves him, even when he is far away from this idyllic place: 'While I stand on the roadway, or on the pavements grey,/I hear it in the deep heart's core.'*

Try to make your vocabulary varied and interesting. Whenever possible, you should avoid repetition. Practice makes perfect here:

use a dictionary and a thesaurus when you are doing your homework. If you are tempted to use lots of qualifying words such as 'very' or 'fairly' or 'really', it is worth taking a moment to see if you can think of a more appropriate word or words. Too many qualifiers weaken your writing. For example, rather than saying, 'The story was very good,' you could say, 'The story was enthralling.'

When answering on a text, remember not to add any opinions of your own, or any facts you might know which are not in the text, unless you are explicitly asked to do so. All the answers must be based on the text. You will have plenty of opportunity to express yourself in the Personal Writing section.

If you are asked for your own opinion, don't be afraid to be honest and say what you really think about the text, provided you can justify your view and back it up with relevant quotations or references.

TYPES OF WRITING

The Junior Cert will test your ability to recognise features of various types of writing and will also require you to show that you can use the appropriate style of writing for the task you are set. This is particularly important in the Personal Writing and Functional Writing sections of Paper 1.

Remember, styles of writing can overlap. A speech writer may include facts and figures or other pieces of information, and may also use humorous anecdotes to keep the audience entertained. Most narrative writing will include plenty of descriptive writing.

Writing to inform – Key Features

- The information is given in a clear, straightforward way.
- The writing is objective; we do not know the writer's own opinion on the topic.
- Facts and figures are given.

The word 'I' is rarely used in informative writing. Adjectives and adverbs are used sparingly as they can make the writing subjective. Look at your Geography textbook, for example. There is a lot of information there, but you know nothing about the opinions of the person who wrote the book. Think of the difference between the way a place is described in a textbook and a tourist guide. Compare these brief descriptions of the Lee Valley in Cork:

> *The Lee Valley stretches from the Derrynasaggart Mountains on the Cork/Kerry border to Cork Harbour. The two main rivers which flow through the valley are the Lee and the Sullane.*
>
> (Informative and objective)
>
> *The beautiful Lee Valley stretches from the unspoilt mountains on the Cork/Kerry border to Cork Harbour. The whole area is rich in fascinating history and teeming with wonderful wildlife.*
>
> (Descriptive and subjective)

It is difficult to make a piece written in the language of information gripping, particularly if the subject matter is one in which your reader has very little interest. Don't assume that the hobby you enjoy will be equally riveting to others.

Writing to argue, debate or make a case – Key Features

In this type of writing, also known as discursive writing, the writer presents a viewpoint and tries to win the reader over to his or her opinion.

Rhetorical questions (questions to which an answer is not expected or an argument phrased in the form of a question to which there is only one possible answer) are commonly used to engage the reader and to try to make him or her believe that there is a conversation taking place between the writer and the reader. They can also make the reader think about the points being raised.

Using rhetorical questions cleverly avoids giving the reader the impression that he or she is on the receiving end of a lecture. If people feel they are being lectured to, they may decide that the writer is arrogant, and the writer may lose their support.

Rhetorical questions can be a good way to start a speech or talk as they capture the reader's interest immediately. Look at the following example from the opening of a speech about chain emails:

> *Did you know that Facebook has become so overpopulated that if you don't log on within the next twelve hours your account will be deleted in an effort to free up some space? And have you heard that Facebook is planning to charge users for uploading photos and comments in the same way that your mobile phone company charges you for texts? No? Well, you'd better forward these messages on to all your friends as quickly as possible, in case they haven't heard either.*
>
> *Of course, neither of these claims is true. But they are typical of the sort of nonsense that is passed around every day on the internet. These are fairly harmless spam messages, but there are other, far more unpleasant and potentially dangerous emails being forwarded by those who should know better.*

Facts and figures are given, but they are carefully chosen to support the point the writer is making. Using statistics can make the writer's case seem well-researched and therefore more credible.

Acknowledging that there are other viewpoints can be helpful if it is done correctly. This can be an effective technique as it makes the writer appear rational and fair-minded. The writer may anticipate and briefly respond to the reader's possible objections to the argument, but should not weaken the case by giving both sides of the argument equal weight.

> *There are, of course, those who say that if schools do not have uniforms, students will be distracted by the fashions and*

accessories sported by their classmates and will not concentrate on their work. I feel that this is a ridiculous argument which implies that teenagers are immature, shallow and silly. As we all know, this is not the case.

Quotations can give the impression that the writer is just one of many people who feels this way about the topic under discussion. A quote can be a good way to begin or end a piece of discursive writing.

I hope that I have succeeded in impressing upon you all the need to begin studying in September and not to wait until the panic and pressure sets in after the mock exams. Leaving things until the last minute is never a good idea. In the words of Benjamin Franklin, 'By failing to prepare, you are preparing to fail.'

There are certain words and phrases which make the reader feel that they, and everybody else, have always agreed with the statement being made. The information now takes on the appearance of being a well-known, established fact. The reader feels that if he or she does not agree with the statement, he or she is in a minority. Use of the word 'we' can also help to make the reader or listener feel on the same side as the speech writer. Here are some examples:

Clearly, plainly, undoubtedly, obviously, surely, as we all know ..., everybody is fully aware that ...

Repetition can add emphasis: 'We must act, and we must act quickly.'

Antithesis is the contrast of ideas by means of a parallel arrangement of words. This might sound complicated, but all it means is using the same words in a slightly different order to create a completely contrasting idea. Look at this example from John F. Kennedy's inaugural speech: *'Let us never negotiate out of fear, but let us never fear to negotiate.'* And, of course, there is also JFK's famous, *'Ask not what your country can do for you, but what* *you can do for your country.'* Such sentences are memorable, which is exactly what you want when you are trying to win someone over to your point of view.

Emotional manipulation can play on the reader's conscience, making him or her feel guilty or pressurised into agreeing with the case being made. It can also flatter the reader into agreeing, and it is a common technique in advertising: 'As a discerning customer, we know you want nothing but the best.' Think of the L'Oréal campaign in which we are constantly told that we are 'worth it'.

Personal opinion and anecdotes are often used to support the point being made. (An anecdote is a short account of something interesting or amusing, often drawn from the writer's own experience.) For example, someone writing a talk to advise Junior Cert students on how to prepare for their exam may well tell stories about their own student days and what they found helpful or otherwise.

Narrative writing – Key Features

The purpose of narrative writing is to inform or entertain the reader. It is the type of writing most people use when they first write personal essays. In narrative writing, you are simply telling a story. The story may be fact or fiction.

The text or texts you have studied for the Studied Fiction section of Paper 2 are examples of narrative writing.

Most stories follow a similar pattern:

- The characters, the place and the time in which the story is set are established.
- We learn of a complication or complications which will affect the characters.
- The characters react to the complications.
- There is a climax, or moment of highest tension, when everything comes to a head and a resolution must be found.

- There is a resolution and we learn of its effect on the characters.
- There may be a moral or a lesson to be learned from the events that have taken place.

Narrative writing usually contains elements of descriptive writing to add atmosphere and give us a better picture of the characters and the setting.

An autobiographical narrative is a true story about an event or events in the writer's life. The events are usually described in the order in which they occurred (chronological order) and the writer gives his or her opinions on the events.

Descriptive writing – Key Features

While it is more usually associated with fiction, descriptive language can also be used in non-fiction. Good examples of descriptive language can be found in books and magazines on travel or nature.

Events and places are **described in detail**.

Adjectives and adverbs are used to make the writing more vivid. Adjectives are words which tell us more about nouns: 'the **large, black** dog'. Adverbs are words which tell us more about verbs: 'he ran **quickly**' or 'she shouted **loudly**'.

Personification (giving human qualities to inanimate objects) can also be used to make the writing more vivid and it can add to the atmosphere of the piece: 'The wind howled angrily around me and tugged at my clothes.'

Descriptive writing **appeals to the senses**. If a reader can imagine the sights and sounds, he or she will be engaged by the writing. Look at the following example from the Unseen Fiction section of the 2003 Junior Certificate exam:

It had been drizzling steadily since the first grey shadows of dawn had crept over the city, and the lanes and alleyways around

Spitalfields market were glistening with rain and vegetable refuse. The great steel barn of the fruit market echoed with the shouts of porters, the whinings of forklift trucks, the crashing of crates and the tramp of feet.

Think of the terminology you learned for your poetry section.

Metaphors and similes are used to good effect in descriptive writing. 'He ran like lightning.' 'She was a silly goose.'

The language can be musically pleasing, as in a poem. Just as in poetry, alliteration and assonance can be used in prose to create a sense of atmosphere. Look at the following sentence from James Joyce's *The Dead:*

> *His soul swooned slowly as he heard the snow falling faintly through the universe and faintly falling, like the descent of their last end, upon all the living and the dead.*

The repeated 's' sounds add to the sense of peace and silence and the repetition of the alliterative words 'faintly' and 'falling' mimic the relentless snowfall.

Humorous writing – Key Features

- The writer may deliberately exaggerate the facts of a story for comic effect.
- There may be humorous misunderstandings, where the reader knows all the facts, but the characters don't.
- The writer may present things to us in a way we would not expect.
- Comparisons can be used to good effect here.
- The writer may be self-deprecating. This simply means speaking about oneself in a modest or critical manner, usually for comic effect.

This edited extract from the book *U2 BY U2* was part of the Reading Section in the 2010 Junior Certificate exam and it contains many of the features of humorous writing which are given above. The author is **self-deprecating**, he deliberately **exaggerates** his ugliness for comic effect, and he **compares** himself to a famously ugly cartoon character.

I was a very cute toddler; I've seen the photographs. But then at around the age of five something started to happen that radically changed my appearance. We are not talking here about some accidental injury or anything medical, but a gradual transformation. My appearance started to inspire a certain mild alarm in adults who caught sight of me for the first time and to elicit sympathetic and vaguely disappointed looks from my parents. My head grew, quite quickly, to an unfeasibly large size. It was not a disagreeable head, in certain contexts it was quite handsome, but from the age of five as a result of this unusual development I started to look unnervingly like the kid on the cover of *Mad* magazine. Along with the head came the teeth, or specifically my two big front teeth. No matter what form of mouth management I employed, there was just no hiding them, so by the time I was seven the full *Mad* magazine look was complete.

Autobiographical writing – Key Features

- An autobiography is a story of a person's life, written by that person.
- It is written in the first person: 'I remember the first time I saw …'
- It is a personal account of the writer's life. We usually get a good sense of the writer's personality from reading their autobiography.
- It gives us insights and information that we would not otherwise have. For example, we might read about a celebrity's feelings on winning an Oscar, or a sportsperson's emotions on taking Olympic gold.
- The writing will be subjective. The person writing the autobiography will naturally want to give their perspective on the events described. Some famous people write autobiographies as a way of offering a defence for behaviour that may have been badly received by the public. This is their chance to tell their side of the story.
- Autobiographies can be nostalgic. The writer may look back fondly at days long gone.

The 2010 Reading section of Paper 1 is an example of auto-biographical writing. It is printed in full in the Reading chapter of this book (page 29).

Dramatic writing – Key Features

Think of the play or plays you have studied for the Drama section of Paper 2. Those plays are examples of dramatic writing.

- There may be a brief introduction and a concluding paragraph.
- In dialogue, each speaker is given a new line. There is no need to use quotation marks. The speaker's name is put at the start of the line, followed by a colon.

- Stage direction may be used. This can add to the atmosphere and help the reader to imagine the characters and the events in more detail.

In the following example from the 2010 Junior Certificate exam we see how brief but revealing stage directions help us to imagine not only the set but also the tone of voice certain characters use:

The following extract (in edited form) is adapted from the play Same Old Moon *by Geraldine Aron.*

Background to this extract

In this extract we meet Brenda Barnes, just home from Australia. She is visiting her widowed mother Bridie and her Aunt Peace, who live together.

Also on stage we see the ghost of Desmond, Bridie's late husband and Brenda's father. Although he reacts to the women's conversation, Desmond says nothing during this extract.

1980s. The stage is split in two – a small cramped living room and a bedroom section which is occupied by Desmond's ghost. The ghost reacts from time to time but is generally still and inconspicuous. Bridie has prepared a tea-trolley; she enters with the milk jug, and puts it on the trolley

BRENDA: New curtains, Mum? They're lovely.

BRIDIE: Thanks, love.

PEACE: I was just thinking to myself that if you weren't going to notice them we'd wasted our time making them. I thought you'd say something the minute you came in.

BRENDA: *(Reasonably)* Give us a chance. I mean they don't exactly jump out at a person. They're exactly the same as the old ones … *(Uncertainly)* aren't they?

BRIDIE: These are mushroom. The old ones were beige. We might as well have kept them if you can't see the difference. Well, I must say Brenda, I thought you were more observant. Not a word about the new tea-trolley.

(Bridie hands out cups of tea, first to Peace, then to Brenda)

BRIDIE: Here we are now. Sugar's in.

READING

*The Reading section of Paper 1 is worth **40 marks**.*

*You should spend about **35 minutes** on this section.*

MARKING ✓

Total: **40**

This is the first section in Paper 1 and it is a good idea to answer the Reading questions first as they can help you in your approach to the rest of the exam. You might pick up ideas for your Personal Writing task, for example, from your reading of the text. At the very least, answering questions on the Reading Comprehension will get you writing, and that is the most important thing.

TYPES OF QUESTION

In this section, you might be asked about:

- Your understanding of the piece. Look out for the word 'what' here, and remember, the answer is on the page in front of you.
- The style in which the piece is written. The word 'how' will often give you a clue that the question is about style.
- What you have learned about the character of the writer or another person in the text.
- Why the author is writing this piece. Is it to inform, or to make a case for or against something, for example? Or is the writer's intention to share childhood memories with us?
- Your opinion of the piece. Stick to the text in your answer.

Questions on style

Questions on style can appear off-putting to students, but with a little practice they can be among the easiest questions on the

'A house without books is like a room without windows.'
– Horace Mann

paper. They can appear in the Reading section in Paper 1, and in the Poetry and Fiction sections in Paper 2. There will be slight differences in the way the questions are phrased, but the main thing to remember is that you are generally being asked to comment on how the writer presents the material and what effect this has on you as a reader. It is important to be aware of the main types of writing and to recognise which type (or types) the writer is using in the text. The key features of these different writing styles are detailed in the previous section of this book. As well as being able to identify these features, you must be able to say what they do. You may be asked whether you find the writer's style effective and you must remember to explain your answer. To do this, you must use a verb to explain what each feature does. For example: 'The writer's use of rhetorical questions **engages** the reader and **provokes thought** on the topic being discussed.'

Here are some examples of the way questions on style have been phrased in past exams.

- This passage is written in an autobiographical style. Identify two aspects of this style evident in the passage and comment on their effect on you as a reader. (2010 Reading)
- Did you find this passage entertaining? Give reasons for your answer. (2006 Reading)
- Do you like the way this extract is written? (2008 Unseen Fiction)
- How does the poet convey a sense of excitement about the water in the poem? (2009 Unseen Poetry)

WRITING YOUR ANSWER

You should spend about 35 minutes on this section, which is worth 40 marks.

It is a good idea to jot down a brief plan for your answer. This need not be neat and should not take you more than a couple of minutes. Look carefully at the question before deciding how many points you are going to make in your answer. If, for example, you are asked to point out and discuss two features of the writer's style, then you will probably only need to write two paragraphs. If there is no guideline as to how many points you should make, use your common sense. Look at the marks awarded for each question. If the question is worth five marks, one paragraph will be sufficient.

Read the Exam Tips section at the start of this book (page 12) for more details on how to approach your answer.

SECTION 1, **PAPER 1, JUNIOR CERT HL, 2010**

Read carefully the following passage and then answer the questions that follow.

The following edited extract is from the book *U2 BY U2*, written by band members Bono, The Edge, Adam Clayton and Larry Mullen with Neil McCormick.

The book tells the story of this highly successful Irish rock band. In this extract band member The Edge (David Evans), talks about his youth and his introduction to music.

I was a very cute toddler; I've seen the photographs. But then at around the age of five something started to happen that radically changed my appearance. We are not talking here about some accidental injury or anything medical, but a gradual transformation. My appearance started to inspire a certain mild alarm in adults who caught sight of me for the first time and to elicit sympathetic and vaguely disappointed looks from my parents. My head grew, quite quickly, to an unfeasibly large size. It was not a disagreeable head, in certain contexts it was quite handsome, but from the age of five as a result of this unusual development I started to look unnervingly like the kid on the cover of *Mad* magazine. Along with the head came the teeth, or specifically my two big front teeth. No matter what form of mouth management I employed, there was just no hiding them, so by the time I was seven the full *Mad* magazine look was complete.

The Edge as a boy alongside the popular US magazine

This was made all the more difficult by the fact that my best friend Shane Fogarty, a person from whom I was pretty much inseparable from the age of two, was like a good-looking actor complete with cornflower-blue eyes and perfect teeth. He knew it, as did everybody else. A year older than me, Shane was super-popular, a great athlete and in many ways my nemesis*. It's funny how even as a young kid you pick up on these things. I went through some very formative years as the proverbial ugly duckling with my mate Shane a constant reminder that I was nothing special. The upshot was that I grew even more shy and awkward. I think that kind of experience is either the making or the breaking of you. And in my case having a very supportive home life helped a lot, but I didn't see that at the time.

The Edge as a rock star

Music was big in our house. When I was two my mother used to turn on the TV so I could play drums (knitting needles and a few biscuit tins) along to the soundtrack. My mother must have suspected I had an ear for music because she bought me a little Spanish guitar when I was seven years old. For me, this was completely fascinating. I couldn't tune it, I didn't even know how to hold it, but it was so cool – that much I did know. I would wave it around and pretend to the gullible youngsters on our street that I could play. That first guitar of mine was really little more than a toy. The first proper guitar that came into our house was bought by my mother at a jumble sale for a pound. Never in the history of the Malahide parish bring-and-buy sales has one pound been as well spent, and given back as much value. It was rough, but it played in tune, and when we replaced the rusty wire strings with some nylon Spanish guitar strings it sounded decent enough.

I learnt my first chords on that guitar, tutored very effectively by my brother Richard, and pretty soon I started working out how to play whole songs. My brother and I always had a very close rapport, and very similar sense of humour and general outlook. I was interested to discover that I could do a lot with that instrument, and I drove everyone in the house mad by playing it at all times, while doing all manner of other tasks. I could eat toast and play guitar, get dressed without missing a note. I would play along every evening while the family watched TV, providing a kind of silent-movie-era soundtrack. My poor mother gave up shouting at me to stop.

It is hard to explain the significance of music for all of the kids in our area. There was nothing else nearly as important in terms of establishing your identity. I would have huge arguments with my friends about who was the best band in the world, or what was the best record ever made. The TV music shows *Top of the Pops* and *The Old Grey Whistle Test* were considered unmissable. The British music papers *NME* and *Sounds* were read from cover to cover, mostly courtesy of our friend Fergus Crossan who had a part-time job and could afford such luxuries. Another friend, David 'Barney' Barnett, told me he was in a band. When I went over to his house and saw him drumming with his band I was absolutely stunned. I knew I had to get into a band. I felt like I had found my niche.

Nemesis – an opponent who cannot be beaten or overcome

Answer the following **three** questions:

1. Trace the growing importance of music during the course of Edge's youth. Support your answer with reference to the text. (10 marks)

2. Basing your answer on evidence from the passage, do you think Edge was a happy teenager? (15 marks)

3. This passage is written in an autobiographical style. Identify two aspects of this style evident in the passage and comment on their effect on you as a reader. (15 marks)

Note: In the exam paper, Dave Evans is referred to as 'Edge'. He is also known as 'The Edge', so either name would be fine in your answer.

Sample Answer 1

1. Trace the growing importance of music during the course of Edge's youth. Support your answer with reference to the text. (10)

This question requires you to focus on the growing importance of music in Edge's youth. Therefore, you must make sure to trace the steps that led to music becoming more and more important in his life as he grew up. However, you must also be sure to refer back to the question in your answer. If you simply list examples of music in Edge's life you will get a low grade.

Look at the marks awarded for this question. There are ten marks, so you should not spend as much time on this question as you would on the other two.

Don't rely on your memory. Scan each paragraph quickly and underline the relevant points. (It can be a help to have different coloured pens or highlighters with you in the exam so that you can use separate colours to underline the sections relevant to the different questions. Otherwise, by the time you get to the final question, much of the Reading Comprehension may be underlined and you may not know which section relates to which question.) In this extract, the references to music only begin at the start of the third paragraph.

There are three paragraphs dealing with the growing importance of music in Edge's youth. This is helpful, as you can write three short paragraphs in your own answer, based on a summary of the main points in each of the paragraphs in the extract.

The answer is in chronological order, starting with Edge's early childhood and moving on, all the while emphasising the fact that music was becoming a bigger part of his life as he grew older

Music was important in Edge's life from a very early age. At the age of two he used knitting needles and biscuit tins to play along with music soundtracks on the TV. Realising that her son had an ear for music, Edge's mother bought him a small Spanish guitar when he was seven. Although he couldn't play it, he thought it was 'cool'.

When he got his first 'proper guitar', Edge became even more interested in music. His brother taught him how to play and Edge played it 'at all times', even while doing other tasks such as eating or getting dressed. He played incessantly and what had been an interest now seemed to be almost an obsession.

Each point is supported by reference to the text

As he grew older, music took over almost every part of Edge's life. He says that it was a way of establishing identity for the kids in his area. They pored over music magazines, watched music TV and argued over which band was best. One of his friends played in a band, and when Edge saw them perform he was 'stunned'. He knew then that he had to join a band too. He felt that he had found his 'niche', which implies that music was by now the main focus of his life.

The answer regularly refers to the growing importance of the role of music in Edge's life

Sample Answer 2

2. Basing your answer on evidence from the passage, do you think Edge was a happy teenager? (15)

You could agree or disagree with the statement. There is no right or wrong answer here, as long as you support your points with quotation from or reference to the passage.

Remember to focus on Edge's teenage years only. His early childhood is not relevant to this question.

I think Edge was a happy teenager. He writes humorously and affectionately about his youth in Dublin and his tolerant and 'very supportive' family. For example, his mother fostered her teenage son's interest in music by buying him an old but serviceable guitar at a jumble sale and his brother tutored him 'very effectively'. Edge also says that he had a 'very close rapport' with his brother and this must have contributed to a happy atmosphere at home. Even the occasions when his mother shouted at him for his constant guitar playing are recalled with understanding and fondness when Edge says, 'My poor mother gave up shouting at me to stop.' The use of the adjective 'poor' to describe his mother shows that Edge did not mind her shouting at him, but sympathised with her frustration at his constant strumming on the guitar.

He talks about the times he spent with his friends while they chatted about music, watched TV and read magazines. The impression he gives is that he was part of a large group of young people who all shared an interest in music. Such connections would undoubtedly help to make Edge's teenage years enjoyable ones.

The opening sentence immediately answers the question

Examples from the text support the view that Edge was a happy teenager

Whether at home or out with his friends, Edge seems to have been surrounded by like-minded people with whom he could share his greatest passion. We know from the introduction, and from general knowledge, that Edge is now a highly successful musician and that he regarded joining a band as finding his 'niche', so it is likely that the music-filled teenage years he describes in this extract would have made him very happy indeed.

Final sentence links back to the question and ties up the answer neatly

Sample Answer 3

3. This passage is written in an autobiographical style. Identify two aspects of this style evident in the passage and comment on their effect on you as a reader. (15)

You are asked to identify **two** features of style, which means you will be writing two paragraphs. In each one, you must comment on the effectiveness of the stylistic features you have chosen.

Refer back to the section on autobiographical writing (page 23) if you need to revise the key features of this style.

The first paragraph focuses on the subjective, personal nature of Edge's autobiographical piece

This autobiographical narrative is a subjective look back at the writer's formative years. Edge moves chronologically through the events which led to his joining a band and becoming a professional musician. Edge's recollection of his childhood in Dublin is engaging and interesting because it is quite personal. It gives us an insight into Edge's own feelings about his upbringing and tells us things that we would be unlikely to learn from anyone else. For example, while we might know that Shane Fogarty was a close friend of his, the fact that Edge felt like 'an ugly duckling' in the other boy's presence and that he regarded Shane as a 'nemesis' in many ways is something a biographer might not know. I found it very interesting to hear such intimate and honest details from the man himself. Had they been written by someone else, I might have doubted their authenticity.

The question asked that you comment on the effectiveness of the style. This means you must say what it meant to you and whether you liked or disliked it

Edge also reflects on the way in which his upbringing affected him and made him the person he is today. This is not simply a dry account of the events in his childhood or a nostalgic look back through his early years; it is an attempt to put those years into context. Edge does not just tell us that feeling ugly and believing he was 'nothing special' was a constant part of his school-days, but he says that he has come to realise that such an experience is 'either the making or the breaking of you'. He is able, with the benefit of hindsight, to appreciate that having 'a very supportive home life helped a lot', even if he 'didn't see that at the time'. This reflection added depth to the writing and helped to tie all the anecdotes together. I enjoyed reading this extract because I felt that it gave me an understanding of how one of the most famous musicians in this country was shaped by the relationships he had with family and friends.

The second paragraph focuses on Edge's ability to look back on those years and reflect on their importance in his life

SECTION 1, PAPER 1, JUNIOR CERT HL, 2008

Read carefully the following passage and then answer the questions that follow.

The following is an extract from the journal of the naturalist, Charles Darwin, in which he recorded his research and observations into the natural history and geology of the countries visited during the voyage of the H.M.S. *Beagle* round the world under the command of Captain FitzRoy, R.N.

Charles Darwin's Journal

After having been twice driven back by heavy southwestern gales, Her Majesty's Ship, *Beagle,* a ten-gun brig, under the command of Captain FitzRoy, R.N., sailed from Devonport on the 27th of December 1831. The object of the expedition was to complete the survey of Patagonia and Tierra del Fuego, begun by Captain King in

1826 and continuing until 1830; to survey the shores of Chile, Peru, and of some islands in the Pacific; and to carry a chain of chronometrical measurements round the World. On the 6th of January we reached Tenerife, but were prevented from landing by fears of our bringing the cholera. The next morning we saw the sun rise behind the rugged outline of the Grand Canary Island, suddenly illuminating the Peak of Tenerife whilst the lower parts of the island were veiled in fleecy clouds. This was the first of many delightful days never to be forgotten. On the 16th of January, 1832, we anchored at Porto Praya, in St. Jago, the chief island of the Cape de Verd archipelago.

Charles Darwin

The neighbourhood of Porto Praya, viewed from the sea, wears a desolate aspect. The volcanic fires of a past age and the scorching heat of a tropical sun have, in most places, rendered the soil unfit for vegetation. The country rises in successive steps of table-land, interspersed with some truncate conical hills, and the horizon is bounded by an irregular chain of more lofty mountains. The scene, as beheld through the hazy atmosphere of this climate, is one of great interest – if, indeed, a person, fresh from sea, and who has just walked, for the first time, in a grove of cocoa-nut trees, can be a judge of anything but his own happiness. The island would generally be considered as very uninteresting, but to any one accustomed only to an English landscape, the novel aspect of an utterly sterile land possesses a grandeur which more vegetation might spoil. A single green leaf can scarcely be discovered over wide tracts of the lava plains; yet flocks of goats, together with a few cows, contrive to exist. It rains very seldom, but during a short portion of the year heavy torrents fall, and immediately afterwards a light vegetation springs out of every crevice. This soon withers, and upon such naturally formed hay the animals live. It had not now rained for an entire year.

When the island was discovered, the immediate neighbourhood of Porto Praya was clothed with trees, the reckless destruction of which has caused here, as at St. Helena, and at some of the Canary islands, almost entire sterility. The broad, flat-bottomed valleys, many of which serve during a few days only in the season as watercourses, are clothed with thickets of leafless bushes. Few living creatures inhabit these valleys. The commonest bird is a kingfisher *(Dacelo Iagoensis)*, which tamely sits on the branches of the castor-oil plant, and thence darts on grasshoppers and lizards. It is brightly coloured, but not so beautiful as the European species. In its flight, manners, and place of habitation – which is generally in the driest valley – there is also a wide difference.

H.M.S. **Beagle**

Another day we rode to the village of St. Domingo, situated near the centre of the island. On a small plateau, which we crossed, a few stunted acacias were growing; their tops had been bent by the steady trade wind in a singular manner, some of them even at right angles to their trunks. The direction of the branches was exactly northeast by north, and southwest by south, and these natural vanes must indicate the prevailing direction and the force of the trade winds. The travelling had made so little impression on the barren soil that we here missed our track to Fuentes. This we did not find out till we eventually arrived there. Fuentes is a pretty village, with a small stream; and everything appeared to prosper well, excepting, indeed, that which ought to do so most – its inhabitants.

When morning came the view was clear; the distant mountains being projected with the sharpest outline onto a heavy bank of dark blue clouds. Judging from the appearance, and from similar cases I had observed in England, I supposed that the air was saturated with moisture. The fact, however, turned out to be quite the contrary. The hygrometer gave a difference of 29.6 degrees between the temperature of the air, and the point at which dew was precipitated. This difference was nearly double that which I had observed on the previous mornings. This unusual degree of atmospheric dryness was accompanied by continual flashes of lightning. Is it not an uncommon case thus to find a remarkable degree of clear dry air in attendance with such action of lightning?

*Answer the following **three** questions:*

1. Darwin had an eye for detail. Briefly discuss this view with reference to the passage. (10 marks)

2. Despite being written in 1832 much of the content of the passage is of interest to modern readers. Do you agree? Explain your point of view with detailed reference to the text. (15 marks)

3. Would you like to have accompanied Darwin on his voyage? Give reasons for your answer based on evidence from the text. (15 marks)

Sample Answer 1

1.   Darwin had an eye for detail. Briefly discuss this view with reference to the passage. (10)

As this question is worth 10 marks, it would be advisable to make **two well-developed points** and to give each point a new paragraph. The paragraphs need not be long, but each should be supported by suitable quotations from the text.

    Note that the wording of the question requires you to make

'reference to the passage'. This is essentially a question about style, and about descriptive style in particular. Refer back to the section on different writing styles in Chapter 1 (page 15) to help you revise for this answer.

This answer is slightly longer than you would be expected to write for a ten-mark question in the exam, but it is no harm to see how a point can be well developed and a point of view supported by close reference to the text.

Darwin's eye for detail can be seen clearly in this extract from his journal. Before he even steps ashore he is taking note of the island as 'viewed from the sea' and he paints a vivid picture of the landscape for us. His use of adjectives adds accuracy and interest to his writing. For example, in one sentence alone he describes the stepped 'table-land', the 'truncate conical hills' and the 'irregular chain of more lofty mountains'. His chosen adjectives are both precise and atmospheric. The word 'lofty' gives us the impression not just of the mountains' height, but also of their impressive quality as they rise above the smaller hills.

It is not just in his descriptions of the landscape that Darwin shows his ability to write in an accurate, scientific and yet poetic way. His observations on the fauna of the island are equally thorough. He gives us the full, scientific name for the kingfisher – Dacelo Iagoensis – and then goes on to say that it sits 'tamely' on the branch before it 'darts' on its prey. This use of adverb and verb shows how carefully Darwin records the bird's habits and mannerisms and how accurately he can portray its behaviour. Yet his eye for detail contains an element of subjectivity which makes it even more evocative for the reader. He says that the kingfisher is 'not so beautiful' as the European species. Such a comment shows what a keen observer Darwin is and how strongly he feels about the subjects of his observations. He does not merely note the physical aspects of the land and of its inhabitants, but shares with us every detail which might appeal to any of our senses.

Opening sentence reflects the wording of the question

The language of the extract is examined and examples given to support each point made

The point being made here is that detail need not be merely informative but can be descriptive as well. When an example is given, the reason for its choice is fully explained

The conclusion links back to the question by mentioning the word 'detail'. This helps to support the points being made

Sample Answer 2

2. Despite being written in 1832 much of the content of the passage is of interest to modern readers. Do you agree? Explain your point of view with detailed reference to the text. (15)

You must argue your case here and defend your opinion. You are free to agree or disagree. However, as a general rule, it is a good idea to write favourably about the pieces chosen for inclusion in the examination papers. Remember, they are chosen as good examples of their genre, and if you want to criticise them you should be sure that your own English is up to scratch. Positive writing tends to read better than negative writing.

This question is worth 15 marks, so you should try to make **three well-developed points**.

State your point of view in the opening sentence

I agree that much of the content of this passage is of interest to modern readers.

Darwin's interest in nature and in man's impact on our environment is something that is very topical at the moment. He talks about the 'reckless destruction' of the trees around Porto Praya and says that their absence has caused 'almost entire sterility' in the area. I believe that modern readers would be both shocked and interested to learn that not only was environmental damage occurring on such a scale in the 1830s but that it was being condemned even then.

Link is made between the content of the passage and modern concerns

The islands Darwin mentions in this extract would, I feel, be more familiar to modern readers than they would have been to their ancestors. Most people nowadays travel far more widely than their nineteenth-century counterparts did. I believe that modern travellers would be interested to hear the Cape Verde islands described in a way that is at once familiar and strange. These places are now holiday destinations but in Darwin's day they were exotic places that few of his countrymen and countrywomen would have seen.

This passage is relevant to anyone who has even a passing interest in history, travel or ecology. To be able to read Darwin's own account of his travels is a privilege that would appeal to many people, even in this day and age. His writing may appear old-fashioned in places, but it is ultimately accessible and very modern in its subject matter. His concerns are concerns that weigh on the minds of many people in the twenty-first century.

Conclusion refers back to the question

Sample Answer 3

3. Would you like to have accompanied Darwin on his voyage? Give reasons for your answer based on evidence from the text. (15)

This type of question can be a little tricky in that it can be tempting for some students to wander from the point and to begin talking about their personal experiences of travel. Remember, this is a question on the extract. Every point you make must be supported by evidence from the text.

If you decide that you would like to have accompanied Darwin on his voyage, be sure to use plenty of words that show enthusiasm: 'wonderful', 'interesting', 'intriguing', etc.

As this is a 15-mark question, you should aim to make **three well-developed points**.

Yes, I would like to have accompanied Darwin on his voyage because I am very interested in nature. It would be wonderful to spend time with someone as keenly observant and curious as Darwin. For example, although I might notice that the day was cloudy, I would be unlikely to take out a hygrometer and test the conditions. Darwin is always questioning, wondering why there is 'a remarkable degree of clear dry air' along with the lightning. I think it would be intriguing to see such a great scientist at work and to learn a little about what makes him tick.

State your position clearly in the opening sentence. Do not make the examiner work it out for themselves

Each point is supported by a quote from the extract

I would also like to sail on the Beagle *because I love to travel. Travel nowadays is a little bit dull in that there is little for the passenger to do but sit in a cushioned seat and try to peer out of a tiny window at the world flashing by. Sailing on a ship in the 1830s would be a fantastic, exciting experience, even if it might be frightening at times to be 'driven back by heavy southwestern gales' as Darwin and his fellow sailors were.*

Above all, though, I think I would like to have accompanied Darwin on his voyage because of how enjoyable he makes it sound. He describes the island of St. Jago in glorious detail and says that he spent 'many delightful days never to be forgotten' there. Who would not want to spend time in such a fabulous place and in the company of such a famous scientist?

PERSONAL WRITING

*The Personal Writing section of Paper 1 is worth **70 marks**.*

*You should spend about **55 minutes** on this section.*

*There is no specified length, but as a general rule you should be aiming to fill approximately **three pages** of your answer book.*

MARKING ✔

Content:	**20**
Structure:	**15**
Expression:	**30**
Mechanics:	**5**
Total:	**70**

Content (ideas, points made)

Your essay should be relevant to the title, have something interesting to say and hold the reader's attention.

Structure

Your essay should be planned, organised and divided into paragraphs, and your ideas should be developed as the writing progresses.

Expression

This is very important. Your writing should be lively and interesting and your vocabulary should be varied.

Mechanics

The examiner will be looking for accurate spelling, grammar and punctuation.

You are free to interpret the titles in any way you choose, unless otherwise stated. This means that you can write in any form you wish, e.g. narrative, descriptive, dramatic, short story and so on. Obviously, if you are told to write a speech or a diary entry or a dialogue between characters, you must use the appropriate writing style. It is a good idea to decide well before the exam which style suits you best and, on the day, pick a title which allows you to write in that style.

Many students are under the impression that they are no good at the Personal Writing section because they do not have a vivid imagination and cannot think up good plots for stories. Nothing could be further from the truth. The Personal Writing section does not require you to make up elaborate and exciting stories, unless that is something you particularly enjoy doing. There are options for everyone.

Whatever type of writing you choose, remember that it is best if it is based at least partly on the truth. You will write more consistently and more credibly if you stick to what you know.

Be realistic. Your essay, were it to be typed out, would probably fill no more than two pages of a book. Some students try to write complicated, elaborate adventure stories in which the action spans many months or even years. This is not a feasible approach. You are far better off describing one event in great detail rather than trying to cram a complicated story into a few pages of writing.

A well-thought-out plan will result in a well-structured essay

The most important thing when writing an essay is to plan. If you do not do this, you will risk writing a badly constructed piece which tails off suddenly or, even worse, ends with, 'I woke up suddenly. It had all been a dream.' Never, ever end an essay this way. Think how cheated you would feel if you were watching a film or reading a book which ended like this with nothing having been resolved. You would demand your money back, and rightly so. An essay which ends this way is a sure sign of an unplanned piece which got out of control. In general, you will need to have a plan for between nine and twelve paragraphs. If you can only think of enough material for four or five paragraphs, consider choosing a different title.

TYPES OF ESSAY

It is important that you know which type of essay suits you best. Between now and the exam, write at least one essay in each of the styles given below. See which ones you are most comfortable with and which ones get you the highest grades. You might surprise yourself!

Narrative writing

Some titles will allow you the opportunity to write about something that happened to you. While the story does not have to be true, it should be based on the truth. Look at this title from the 2010 Personal Writing section: *Write a composition beginning with the lines, 'I was a very cute toddler; I've seen the photographs.'* You could use a story or series of stories from your own life in response to this title.

In order to get a high grade in a narrative essay, you should show the examiner that you can look back at various incidents in your life and reflect on the impact these events had on you.

Most narrative writing will contain elements of descriptive writing. You should refer back to the Chapter 1 of this book and check the key features of both narrative and descriptive writing.

Discursive writing

Discursive writing allows you the opportunity to examine your feelings about the topic you have chosen. You may wish to take a serious or a light-hearted approach. Here is a title from the 2010 examination: *Write a speech for OR against the motion: 'All teenagers should have to participate in sport.'*

Whichever approach you choose, the examiner will reward you for a thoughtful, consistent approach to the topic. You should aim to make four or five strong points in a discursive essay.

Practice makes perfect

If you are thinking of writing a discursive essay, you should keep up with current affairs. Read the newspapers and watch the news on the television.

You should refer to Chapters 1 and 3 of this book to see key features and examples of discursive writing.

The short story

This is one of the most popular choices in the Junior Cert examination, but short stories are very rarely written well. Unlike the personal narrative, this is a piece of fiction and it must follow certain guidelines.

There are a few things you should consider before you attempt a short story.

- You should be prepared to set the scene. However, remember the words of the writer Elmore Leonard, who said, 'I try to leave out the parts that people skip.' Too much description will bore your reader, but too little will make the story unconvincing. It is best, if you can, to work the descriptions of the setting into the fabric of the story rather than giving them a paragraph or more of their own.
- What time span will be covered in the story? It is best if it takes place over a short period of time. Three or four pages of handwriting is not enough to cover many years in a person's life. It is far better to describe a short timeframe in detail than to attempt to span months or years. (It took J.K. Rowling over four thousand pages to tell readers about Harry Potter's years in secondary school!)
- To get a high grade, you need to show how your chosen character copes with conflict. Ideally, he or she needs to experience a life-changing event or learn a valuable lesson.
- It is worth spending some time between now and the examination thinking of a character or characters you might use in your short story. Different types of character raise the possibility of conflict. If you think about your characters now and wonder how they would react in different situations, your writing is likely to be credible and consistent. You can, of course, base characters on people you know, but use your discretion here.

Using dialogue

A good way to start a personal narrative or a short story is to pull the reader in immediately by using dialogue. This can be a great way of getting straight into the plot. You can always supply additional details as you go along to bring your reader up to speed if needs be, but do try to give the reader credit. They will read between the lines if they are engaged by your story.

As a general rule, four or five exchanges is plenty when you are starting an essay. At this point, you should explain what is going on.

Dialogue is a useful tool and can add dramatic effect to your writing, but don't overdo it. It can become dull very quickly.

How to end your composition

It is vital that you end with a good conclusion.

If you are writing a speech, a talk or an article, you may decide to end with a quote or a question.

If you are writing a short story or a personal narrative, you may wish to end with the lesson you or your chosen characters learned. A conclusion is a way of tying up all the ideas in your speech, talk or article. It is not an appropriate time to bring up a new idea.

HOW TO BEGIN?

One of the most difficult things to do is to decide how to begin your essay. If this is something that causes you real trouble time and time again, there are a few things you should consider:

- Choose a speech, diary entry, letter or some other task which clearly defines the form and gives you definite guidelines. Sometimes these are based on the texts or pictures you are given, which can be a great help in kick-starting your writing.
- Choose a title which gives you the opening line.

If you have opted for a title which gives you little or no help, think about the following: *What books have I read lately? Why did I keep reading after the first paragraph?*

If I were telling a friend about something interesting that happened to me at lunchtime, would I start by saying, 'I got up at

half past seven. I jumped out of bed and opened the curtains. It was getting bright, so I got dressed, left the bedroom and went downstairs. I went into the kitchen and put some bread in the toaster. I sat at the table and poured myself a bowl of cornflakes ...'?

You would never tell a story this way as your friend would be screaming at you to get to the point before you had finished the third sentence. The examiner feels much the same way. The approach just shown may be fine for a piece of writing in a foreign language, when you are simply trying to show that you know all the vocabulary for breakfast foods and rooms in the house, but it is far too immature for higher level English. If you decide to write about going to a concert or a match, for example, don't bother telling the examiner all about your journey to the venue. Start when the action starts: 'What had been a steady stream of supporters turned into a pushing, heaving mass by the time we reached the gate ...', or 'A huge roar went up all around me, and I found that I was on my feet too, cheering and shouting along with the rest. The first goal had been scored ...' Then take your story from there.

You have a limited amount of time and space in the exam; don't waste it by describing the weather and your choice of outfit unless these are relevant to the story.

You do not have to write in chronological order. In other words, you can begin at the end of the story, or in the middle, and explain how you ended up in this situation.

Look at the titles below (taken from the 2010 examination) and some of the ways in which each title can be interpreted. These are only guidelines. You may well have better ideas of your own.

Title 1 Music in my life

This title is inspired by the 2010 Reading section, in which The Edge talks about the importance of music in his life. You could base your writing on his style and talk about the growing importance of music in your life since you were a small child.

This might suit students who play an instrument, sing, or are part of a band or choir.

Another approach would be to trace the associations you have with various pieces of music. Think of your summer holidays. Is there a song you associate with a particular place, year or person? What sort of feelings and memories do songs evoke in you? Do you feel a little embarrassed now, remembering your love for certain pieces of music? What about music in your home? Do you like or dislike your family's taste in music?

Write a composition beginning with the lines, 'I was a very cute toddler; I've seen the photographs.'

Title 2

You could write a descriptive piece here, describing yourself during the transition from toddler to teenager. Alternatively, this could be the starting point for a personal essay about yourself in general. You might say that, although you were cute, you were far from well-behaved as a small child. Most of us have stories of terrible things we did as children!

It is important to remember that if you are asked to use the given line or lines in your writing, you must do so.

I was a very cute toddler; I've seen the photographs. I am the eldest in my family, so my parents have album after album devoted to my early years. And in each album, an almost angelic face beams at the camera. No one could guess, looking at that sweet, innocent little face, that I was a complete terror, the bane of my parents' life and a positive menace to any pet foolish enough to wander too close to my chubby, grasping hands. By the age of three I had hugged two budgies to death, popped the cat into the tumble-dryer for a brief spin (he survived, mercifully, but holds a grudge to this day) and smashed almost all my parents' valuable glass and china ...

Sample opening

Title 3 ## The beauty of quiet places

Where do you like to go to escape? Is it a quiet place in the garden, by the sea, or simply the sanctuary of your own room? What about quiet public places? Do you like libraries, galleries or museums? Does the quietness bring you a sense of calm? Are there particular times when you seek solitude or silence? Why? How do such places make you feel?

The chances are that this piece will be quite descriptive and reflective. If you are writing a descriptive piece, try to appeal to as many of the senses as possible.

Sample opening

It is hard, sitting here in the crushing silence of this exam hall, to reflect on the beauty of quiet places. Apart from the occasional rustle of paper, a quickly stifled cough or the scratching of a pen, there is almost total quietness. And it is not a beautiful quietness. I long for noise, for chatter, for laughter. The thought that I have two more weeks of this is almost enough to make me scream aloud. But of course I won't. Not when I'm under the beady eye of the supervisor. She has already looked disapprovingly in my direction, once when I sighed heavily, and once when I inadvertently let my pen roll off the desk and onto the wooden floor.

And yet, if I allow my thoughts to wander, there are quiet places that are far, far more beautiful than this school gym. As soon as the exams are over and I have the opportunity to do so, I am going to go to my favourite of those places. It's a little cove in west Cork, accessible only through a local farmer's fields, and it's the place I love the most. My family prefers to stay in the nearby village with its playground, pub and various amusements, but I cannot wait to head for the tiny, empty cove. As soon as I reach the crest of the hilly fields above it, I can smell the tang of the sea air and seaweed, and I can hear the low booming sound of the waves crashing against the walls of the sea caves that line the

steep shoreline. It's a little piece of heaven and it's all mine.
Nobody else dares or bothers to venture across the half mile or so
of grassland that it takes to get to this blissfully quiet spot. I have
its rock pools and its views all to myself ...

My most useful possessions

Title 4

The danger with an essay like this is that it might simply become a list of your favourite possessions. The examiner will soon tire of reading essay after essay about mobile phones, laptops and all the other gadgets that most people find indispensable.

Try to think around this title a little. How can you interest and surprise the examiner? What is meant by 'useful'? Could you write about something that has genuinely helped you out in difficult situations, even if it's not something glamorous or exciting? Are there things you just could not do without? Why not? Have they a practical use or do they simply make you feel good? Could you write about some useful possessions that are practical and some that are useful because of the way they make you feel? Or could this title be the start of a narrative?

Beep. Beeep. Beeeeeep. There is no sound more strident or more   *Sample opening 1*
irritating than that of my alarm clock. Even thinking about it now
sets my teeth on edge. I detest it. It sits there, smugly, on my
bedside locker, seeming to taunt me with its cheerful vibrancy. It
is an old-fashioned alarm clock and when it rings, it dances
around the surface of the bedside locker, always seeming to be just
out of reach of my groping hand. Bleary-eyed, still half asleep, I
can barely see its outline in the dim light of early morning, let
alone focus enough to hit the right button to turn it off. Every day,
I vow to throw it in the bin.

Yet I never will, because without it I'd be lost. I loathe it and I
love it. It wakes me for school – for which I will not quickly
forgive it – but it also wakes me for early morning flights, for

meetings with friends, for appointments I cannot miss ...

. . . . . .

Sample opening 2   *Phones, iPods, Blackberries, laptops. As I look around the exam hall, I'm sure that many of my fellow students are busily writing about how useful these possessions are. And they are. I do not deny that. I am as guilty of gadget envy as the next person. I want the newest and the shiniest model of mobile phone as soon as it is released. And yet, I could live without all of the things I have listed above. I know for a fact that I could. One unforgettable, terrible weekend camping in the woods last summer taught me that. It also taught me that the most useful possessions I own are a small torch, a length of string and a box of matches ...*

Title 5   You and some friends enter a major talent competition. Write a series of diary entries recording your experiences.

Diary entries are relatively simple to write. All you have to remember is that they are a record of your thoughts and feelings, almost as if you were talking to a close friend, and that you must put the date (and time, if applicable) before each entry.

Sample diary entries   **Friday, 19th May. 10 pm.**

Well, today was action-packed, to say the least. Laura, Michael and I finally decided that the day had come and that we were ready to put the band forward for the competition in June. Talk about leaving it until the last minute! I blame Michael, frankly. He couldn't make up his mind about whether or not he was willing to make what he called 'a show' of himself in public or not. I think he was worried that the lads in his class would laugh at him. Laura and I managed to convince him that anyone who jeered at his guitar playing would only be jealous. It's true. He is very talented, and if anyone lets us down on the night of the competition, it won't be him. It won't be Laura, either. She sings like an angel. Oh, if it all falls apart, it will be my fault, I know it. Laura's voice is far better than mine. The harmonies are fine when we're on our own in Michael's garage, but I don't know how – or even if – it will all sound on the 'Big Night'.

Saturday, 4th June. 7.15 am.

I don't think I have ever been up this early on a Saturday morning. I didn't sleep a wink last night. All I could hear when I laid my head down on the pillow was an endless rendition of our chosen piece. That's hardly surprising, seeing as we have practised it every single day since May. I am heartily sick of the song now, and if I never hear it again after tonight, it will be too soon.

Oh no! What if someone else has chosen that same song as their entry? That never even occurred to me until now. I feel sick at the thought. That's it. Cereal and toast scraped into the dog's bowl. I can't eat. I'm far too nervous.

Saturday, 4th June. 3.45 pm.

Well, it turns out I can eat after all. Uncle Cormac dropped in after breakfast this morning and I ended up pouring out all my woes to him. He listened in silence, then asked if he could hear us perform. I wouldn't have agreed to that if it weren't for the fact that, when he was younger, Uncle Cormac was in a band that released several CDs, one of which went into the top ten for a couple of weeks. Of course, his sort of music is hardly up to date, but still. He has been there and he knows a bit about the recording industry. And frankly, dear diary, I am so desperate now that I would almost listen to advice from my parents. Well, maybe I'm not that desperate yet. I'm still recovering from seeing them dancing at my cousin's wedding last month. No sensitive teenager needs to see her parents making a spectacle of themselves to Justin Timberlake's 'Rock Your Body' ...

Title 6 Write a speech for **or** against the motion: 'All teenagers should have to participate in sport.'

Many students are put off the idea of writing speeches or talks, but they should not be. Read the section on Discursive Writing (page 46) and you will soon see how easy this task can be. You will need to be familiar with this style of writing for your Functional Writing task, so all you need to do for the Personal Writing section is expand upon your ideas a little bit.

This sort of task is especially suited to students who think logically and have strong opinions.

Sample opening 1 – in favour of the motion

We live in a generation where sport is becoming increasingly virtual. We watch television sports channels, we create fantasy football teams, we think that playing Wii tennis games is almost as good as the real thing. But it's not. Our generation is at risk of obesity, heart disease and other ailments, simply because we spend too much time indoors. The couch is no substitute for the court, the pitch, the field or even the local park. So, what can we do about it? Is it too late for us to change our ways? I think not. But I firmly believe that if we are to effect a change, then we must make this change mandatory. That means making sure that each and every teenager in this country should be obliged to take part in some sort of sporting activity at least once a week. And the obvious place to do that is in schools ...

......

Sample opening 2 – against the motion

I have a question for you all. Would you like to continue sitting in this room, listening to a debate about the merits or otherwise of forcing teenagers to participate in sport, or would you like to join me in the park for a game of rounders? It's a sunny afternoon. Sound tempting? I see a few heads nodding. More than a few. But let's change things a little. Instead of asking you if you want to join me, I'm telling you that you have to play rounders. Now. Does that change anything? Has your interest changed to resentment? If so, I'm not at all surprised. Because that is the normal reaction of anyone, adult or teenager, who is told that they must do something. We like choice, particularly as we get older. If we are forced to do something, we are likely to rebel against it and end up disliking it. That's the point I want to make. If we want teenagers to participate in sport, then we have to give them options and allow them some control over their own sporting life ...

A talent I would like to have

Title 7

What talent would you like to have, and why? Is there somebody in your life who inspires you and whose talents you admire? Think about your reasons for wanting the talent you choose. Remember that a lot of students will want to be singers or musicians so that they can become famous. Try to think of something a bit different, and try to surprise the examiner with a fresh approach. Perhaps something happened in your life that made you wish you had a particular talent or ability. This could be the starting point for that story.

If my father and grandfather have green fingers, then I have black fingers. Any plant I touch dies almost immediately. It has become something of a running joke in our family. Along with the usual birthday presents and Christmas presents I get each year, someone always slips a plant into the mix. 'This is indestructible,' they assure me. 'You don't need to do anything except water it once a month.' And yet, long before that month is out, I am looking gloomily at a sad pile of shrivelled leaves.

Sample opening

*   None of this would matter, of course, if it weren't for the fact that our family business is a garden centre and my ambition is to join my father and my grandfather in the business when I leave school. With that in mind, I decided that this would be the year I learned a new talent. I would become better at gardening than*

anyone in my family would ever have thought possible ...

Title 8 Write a story which includes the words, 'I wish I had listened'.

The obvious danger here is that students will write a story which is far too broad in its scope. Teachers and examiners alike have read far too many stories of parties that went wrong and ended up with the house burning down, teenagers who turn to a life of drugs and crime, and other similarly unlikely scenarios. Try to stick to what you know. A simple story, well told, will gain you higher marks than a confused and incredible plot that ends up with you languishing in prison or behind enemy lines in a war zone. Let's face it: most of us have made mistakes at one stage or another, often because we didn't listen to those who were giving us good advice. Some of those mistakes might have had dramatic consequences, some may not.

This title requires you to include the given line in the story, but it does not say where. There is no need to underline or highlight the line when you do use it. The examiner will spot it without your drawing attention to it.

Sample opening 1   *I wish I had listened. 'The wind is picking up,' the woman in the shop had warned. 'If you're thinking of taking that little boat of yours out, I'd wait until later. The mackerel will still be there tomorrow, you know.'*

She meant well, and she had lived by the sea all her life, but of course I didn't pay any attention to her sensible advice. I knew better. And I was impatient to get out to sea and start fishing. I stuffed my purchases – chocolate and bottled water – into my rucksack and almost ran out of the door. Her voice followed me as I carefully negotiated my way down the slippery stone path to the cove ...

'Turn left at the next junction,' droned the old man. 'And then go straight up that hill until you get to the part of the road with no markings ...'

I tuned out. All I had wanted to know was whether or not I was on the right road for Kilmacmichael. If it weren't for the fact that I was so far off the beaten track that I no longer had mobile coverage, I'd have used the sat nav on my phone. Maybe cycling to this campsite hadn't been such a good idea after all. The sun was beginning to dip behind the hills and I had assured my family I'd join them before it got dark.

'That's the most important thing.' I had almost forgotten that the old man was still talking to me. I tried to look alert, feigned gratitude and made to get on my bike once again. He put out a restraining hand and held my arm for a moment. 'Did you get all that?' he asked. I assured him that I had. In truth, I planned to stop again in the next village and either buy a map or ask someone a bit less long-winded for directions.

Now, several hours later, as the darkness seemed to crowd in on me from every side, I stopped once more and peered hopelessly at the vague shapes looming out of the gloom. 'Oh,' I whispered to myself, 'I wish I had listened ...'

FUNCTIONAL WRITING

*The Functional Writing section of Paper 1 is worth **30 marks**. This is the same as the marks allotted to each of the six sections in Paper 2, so it is well worth taking the time to prepare for this task.*

*You should spend about **25 minutes** on this section.*

 MARKING ✔

Total: **30**

You should be prepared to write any of the types of functional writing listed below:

- Letters
- Instructions
- Short speeches or talks
- Reports
- Reviews or 'blurbs' on book jackets/DVD covers
- Newspaper or magazine articles
- Competition entries
- Advertisements
- Picture descriptions

Functional writing means writing for a particular purpose. You are being tested on your knowledge of the accepted layout of things like formal letters, reports and various other types of writing. You are also being tested on your ability to use language in different ways in different circumstances. The examiner will want to see that you can **control** your written English and **adapt** it to suit a variety of tasks.

This is a short piece of writing, not an essay, so keep an eye on the length. There is no hard and fast rule for the length of a Functional Writing piece: it depends on the individual task.

Read the question very carefully and underline the important words.

Think about the target audience for this piece. Who will be reading your writing? It is very important that you write in the correct **register**. This means using language appropriate to the task. If you are writing a letter to your friend, the tone can be chatty and informal; if you are writing a letter to a newspaper or applying for a job, the language must be formal.

Before you start writing, plan what you want to say

Plan your answer very carefully. You may find that the question can help you with this by mentioning things you should include in your letter, report, etc.

Organise your thoughts and express yourself clearly. This is an exercise in communication, so be sure that you are easily understood. Keep your sentences short and simple, particularly if you have a tendency to let your writing get out of control. Before you begin a sentence, know how it is going to end. Don't just start writing and see where it takes you.

There are **four** questions you should ask yourself before beginning your Functional Writing piece:

EXAM FOCUS

1. What **form** will my writing take?
2. What will be the **content** of the piece?
3. Who will my **audience** be?
4. What **register** will I use?

LETTERS

You may be asked to write a formal or an informal letter in the Functional Writing section of Paper 1. Formal letters are far more commonly asked for than informal letters, but it is worth knowing how to write both.

Letter writing – Formal

The most commonly asked formal letters are for the following purposes:

- Writing to a celebrity, telling them why you admire their work
- Applying for a job
- Recommending someone for a particular job
- Inviting someone to an event
- Writing to a newspaper, commenting on a topical issue, often a letter of complaint
- Asking for information

Always use a fictitious (false) name and address when writing a letter in an exam. You should have one ready before the examination; you will have enough to do on the day without trying to think up a false name and address on the spot. The easiest way to do it is to juggle your name and address around a little. You can do the same with the address of your school by using a mixture of your primary and secondary school names and a neighbouring town.

In a formal letter, you may include the recipient's name and job title above the address. You do not have to do this in every circumstance, however. Use your judgement here. You would not have to include a job title if you were writing to a celebrity, but it would be appropriate to do so when writing to a supermarket

Neat handwriting always creates a good impression

manager or any business or professional contact.

Put a comma after each line of the address except the last, which you should end with a full stop.

When you are learning the layout of a formal letter, it is best to be as correct as possible. Some textbooks say you can write the date 02/01/2012, for example, but others disagree. Therefore, it is wise to stick to a format that everybody will find acceptable. You cannot be too correct. The best way to write the date is in the format shown in the letter-writing instructions and the sample answers given in this book.

Letter heading

The address of the letter writer goes in the top right-hand corner.

Line one of your address,	*84 Fountain Court,*
Line two of your address,	*Riverview Road,*
Name of your town or city,	*Athlone,*
County.	*Co. Westmeath.*
Date	*2nd June 2012*

The name, title and address of the person receiving the letter goes on the left-hand side of the page.

Recipient's name,	*Ms Helen Fox,*
Recipient's job title,	*Personnel Manager,*
Line one of recipient's address,	*Great Value Supermarket,*
Line two of recipient's address,	*12 South Circular Road,*
Line three of recipient's address,	*Portobello,*
Recipient's town or city.	*Dublin 8.*

Salutation or greeting

Use the person's title and surname if you know it: 'Dear Mr Murphy'.
If you do not know their name, you may say 'Dear Sir' or 'Dear Madam'.

Dear _____,   *Dear Madam,*

Body of the letter

In the first paragraph you should say why you are writing the letter. Get straight to the point. This is usually a short paragraph. Think of the tone; if you are asking for money, you will want to be persuasive. Ask yourself who will be reading the letter and keep this person in mind throughout. Skip a line before beginning the next paragraph.

In the second paragraph, you should make your next point. Be clear. Make sure you have made a plan and that there is a logical sequence to the paragraphs.

In the third and subsequent paragraphs, you should continue to develop the theme of the letter, giving any facts that you think are relevant. Four or five points should be plenty. Remember to avoid slang, exaggeration, deeply personal anecdotes and any remarks which may be racist, sexist or prejudiced. It is best to avoid contractions in formal letters. For example, you shouldn't write 'I'm' or 'We're'; you should write 'I am' and 'We are' instead.

The final paragraph is usually quite short, thanking the person for taking the time to deal with your complaint or consider your request and so forth. If you would like them to take some action on your behalf, this is the time to ask what they intend to do. You may also tell the recipient to contact you if they have any further queries.

Closing

If you have opened with Dear Sir or Madam
Yours faithfully,

If you do know the recipient's name and have used it
at the start of the letter
Yours sincerely,

Your name, written clearly, appears at the bottom of the letter.
Pat Murphy

*You need a **reference letter** from your Principal to secure a summer job. Write the letter you would like him or her to supply you with. The address you use should not be that of your actual school nor should you use your own name.*
(30 marks)

Note

Underline the key words. It is vital to read the question carefully – you are being asked to write the reference letter, not a letter asking your principal for a reference.

1. **Q** What **form** will my writing take?
   A This will be a formal letter.

2. **Q** What will be the **content** of the piece?
   A The letter will detail your strengths and your suitability for this job.

3. **Q** Who will my **audience** be?
   A The audience will be a potential employer. The type of business is not specified, so you will be free to choose to write to whomever you want, or to write a very general reference letter that could be used for any job.

4. **Q** What **register** will I use?
   A Your language should be formal and precise. You will want the recipient of the letter to employ the student, so you should use persuasive language.

Sample Formal Letter 1

Both addresses given

St Francis College,

Main Street,

Tuam,

Co. Galway.

Date written in full

3rd June 2012

If you don't know the recipient's name you can just use their job title

The Manager,

Castle Hotel,

Tuam,

Co. Galway.

Appropriate salutation. For a general reference letter you could write: 'To whom it may concern'

Dear Sir or Madam,

Orla Hurley has been a pupil at St Francis College since 2008 and, as her principal, I have no hesitation in recommending her for a summer job in your hotel.

Having explained her relationship with the subject of the letter, the writer goes on to list the pupil's attributes. Specific examples are given

Orla is a pleasant, hard-working, co-operative girl who always goes out of her way to help others. Last year, she was chosen by her classmates to be the second-year representative on the Student Council and she undertook this role with diligence and enthusiasm. The majority of the meetings were in the evenings and Orla was unfailingly punctual and reliable. She was asked to take minutes of the meetings on a number of occasions and she showed great initiative in typing up the minutes and distributing them to all the council members the next day.

Example which is relevant to the job – good communication skills are usually required in hotel work

In February of this year, the third-year students were asked to help in organising the Open Day for prospective students' parents and Orla was given the task of preparing and delivering a short talk on her experiences as a pupil in the school. The parents were most impressed with her communication skills and many of them praised her to me later on.

I believe that Orla would be an excellent employee and I am Conclusion
very happy to recommend her for a position in your hotel. If you
require any further information, please do not hesitate to contact
me at the above address.

Yours faithfully, Formal sign-off

Maura Creedon

Maura Creedon
Principal

Letters to the editor

Letters to the editor are similar to normal formal letters: only the layout is different.

There is generally no need to write the editor's name and address at the top of the letter, but you may do so if you wish. Letters to the editor simply begin with 'Sir' or 'Madam', depending on the gender of the editor. Unless the gender of the editor is specified in the Junior Cert question, either opening would be perfectly acceptable.

In your opening sentence, you should give the name, writer and date of the article which prompted you to write the letter. If the letter is a general one, and is not in response to an article which appeared in the paper, you should simply address the topic in the opening lines, for example: 'The issue of exam stress is one which affects almost every student in this country.'

Keep the letter short and to the point. Newspapers do not print long letters which cover several different topics.

You sign off by writing, 'Yours, etc.' rather than 'Yours faithfully,'.

You do not put your name and address at the top of the letter, but at the very end, underneath your signature.

Remember that your audience is the general public. Keep the

tone formal throughout.

Humorous touches are allowed, of course, but be careful here. Not everyone will share your sense of humour.

In 2004, one of the Functional Writing tasks was based on the article printed below. The task was phrased in this way: 'You feel strongly about Hugh Linehan's article in Section 1 of this paper (Page 2). Write a letter to the editor of the newspaper in which you outline your views in response to the article.'

'Call the usher! The pleasure of movie-going is becoming a pain, thanks to noisy, guzzling, mobile phone-using talkers, kickers and general pests.' So said Irish Times *journalist, Hugh Linehan, in an article in his newspaper. The article appears below in edited form.*

Shhhhhhhhh!

Maybe it's because I'm a spoiled snobbish elitist – and that's not something I'm happy about – but I have to confess I'm finding it increasingly painful to go to the movies with the rest of you, the great paying public. It's not because of the cinemas – standards of projection, sound, seating and ventilation have improved out of all recognition over the last ten years – but (and I am sorry to say this) your standards of behaviour seem to be disimproving all the time.

Kickers are a real source of irritation. The kicker problem is exacerbated by the design of modern cinema seats – a kicked seat reverberates right along the row, so that it can be well-nigh impossible to figure out where it's coming from. In the 1970s, they called this Sensurround and people paid to experience it in movies such as Earthquake *and* Towering Inferno. *Nowadays, you can have your own personal towering inferno as you reach boiling point after two hours of bone-shaking juddering.*

Up until recently, the mobile phenomenon seemed to be spinning out of control. Cinemas were buzzing like beehives with the wretched things and some buffoons even had the cheek to strike up conversations on them during the film. There will always be buffoons, but a corner seems to have been turned in recent times. Thankfully, cinemas have now taken to putting reminders on the screen telling people to switch off their phones, and many appear to be doing so. On an electronically related topic, by the way, what sort of benighted fool needs a watch that beeps on the hour, every hour?

I have some sympathy for those who feel nauseated by the smell of warm buttery popcorn, which is so much a part of the multiplex experience, but it doesn't bother me that much. If people want to eat wildly overpriced, grease-saturated cardboard, then that's their business. At least popcorn has the virtue of being (almost) silent food – far better than the high-pitched crackle of the jumbo crisp packet or the extended kitchen-sink gurgle of the almost-drained Coke.

To my mind the real problem in cinemas these days is talkers. They're everywhere and they come in a variety of species. One kind can't help giving a blow-by-blow commentary on the movie. They're bad enough, but there is worse. Top of the list come those who just utterly ignore the film in favour of their own chat. Western society has devised countless places where people can communicate with each other, but cafés, restaurants or street corners are just not good enough for these people – apparently not when they can have the added pleasure of spoiling other people's enjoyment.

Then, there are those who think that any break in the dialogue has been inserted by the film-maker expressly for them to start talking. The minute there is a pause of more than a couple of seconds they launch into conversation. This is not to forget the downright stupid, who spend most of the time asking questions: 'Who's she? What happened there?' By the time they've got an answer they've missed the next plot point, and the whole weary rigmarole starts all over again.

What is the reason for this plague? The general decline in politeness in society may have something to do with it, but it doesn't fully explain the seemingly unstoppable desire to talk when the lights go down. We don't want funereal silence; a good comedy, horror or action movie can be immeasurably improved by the communal experience of seeing it with an audience. People can shriek or laugh to their hearts' content, and there is a real sense of a shared magical experience. After all, we're all together in the cinema … in the dark. And you never know who is sitting next to you!

QUESTION 2, SECTION 3, PAPER 1, JUNIOR CERT HL, 2004

You feel strongly about Hugh Linehan's article in Section 1 of this paper (Page 2). Write a letter to the editor of the newspaper in which you outline your views in response to the article. (30 marks)

1. **Q** What **form** will my writing take?
   A This will be a letter to the editor and should be laid out accordingly.

2. **Q** What will be the **content** of the piece?
   A You may base your comments solely on the original article, or you may draw from your own experience.

3. **Q** Who will my **audience** be?
   A The audience will be anyone who reads the newspaper.

4. **Q** What **register** will I use?
   A Although you may feel strongly about Mr Linehan's article, you must write in a relatively formal way. However, you will be expressing views of your own, so you may wish to attempt to persuade the readers to agree with you.

Sample Letter to the Editor 1

Sir,

In response to Mr Hugh Linehan's article, 'Shhhhhhhhhhh' (April 23rd), I feel I must offer a defence of cinema-goers.

Mr Linehan's arrogant dismissal of other cinema patrons as 'you, the great paying public' is small-minded and unworthy of a journalist writing for a national newspaper. Is he so different from the rest of us that he has to set himself apart and address his readers in this offensive manner?

I was offended by the tone of the opening paragraph, but as I read the rest of the article, I became more bewildered than offended. Why does Mr Linehan complain about mobile phones and then admit that they are not really a problem any more? As for the mention of beeping watches, well, it seems that Mr Linehan is sadly out of touch with the modern world. Those watches went out of fashion quite some years ago.

Mr Linehan's real gripe, though, is against those who dare to talk during the film. While I think most people would agree that incessant chatter is annoying, a night out at the cinema is meant to be a social occasion too, and it's understandable that people might wish to exchange a few words with their friends now and again. It's not the theatre, after all. It's not as if the actors will be disturbed by someone asking their neighbour an occasional question.

It seems to me that Mr Linehan would be better advised to avoid the cinema completely and stay at home with a DVD. I doubt that his fellow cinema-goers would miss his sighs and eye-rolling, nor would any of us miss his subsequent mean-spirited grumbling about what should be a fun, relaxed night out.

Yours, etc.
Fiona Whelan,
15 John Street,
Navan,
Co. Meath.

Sample Letter to the Editor 2

Sir,

I agree wholeheartedly with the sentiments expressed by Mr Hugh Linehan in his article, 'Shhhhhhhhhhh' (April 23rd).

This letter is based on the problems outlined by Hugh Linehan in his article, but it goes on to deal with the issue in a more personal way

My friends and I go to our local cinema once a week and it has become an increasingly unpleasant way to spend an evening, unfortunately. As Mr Linehan points out, the thoughtlessness and bad manners of some cinema-goers ruin the experience for everyone else.

Letters to the editor are often letters of complaint

We have complained to the cinema staff but they seem unwilling or unable to do anything about it. I fail to see why they can't throw the trouble-makers out. Surely, in this age of CCTV, it would be a simple matter to identify the culprits and ban them from entering the cinema again.

Suggesting solutions to the problem is common in such letters

I am grateful to Mr Linehan for raising this topic and I hope that cinema owners and managers will take note. The majority of their income comes from people who want to enjoy watching a film in peace. If the disruptive element is not dealt with, most people will simply choose to wait until new films are released on DVD and watch them in the comfort of their own homes.

The conclusion refers back to the article which prompted the letter

Yours, etc.
Fiona Whelan,
15 John Street,
Navan,
Co. Meath.

Letter writing – Informal

Note

Very few people write informal letters nowadays; instead they write emails. (If you are asked to write an email, the language should be similar to that of an informal letter, but you would not put your address at the top of the page.)

The Old Rectory,
Ballymoat,
Co. Sligo.

Sample sender's address

3rd June 2012

Dear _____,

It is usual to begin the first paragraph directly underneath the comma after the recipient's name. In an informal letter, the tone can be much more relaxed. You may use some slang, but avoid text language and, of course, bad language. If you must use exclamation marks, use them with caution and never use more than one at a time.

The content of an informal letter depends on the person to whom you are writing and the reason for your letter. Use personal stories and try to keep the tone lively and interesting.

You may be telling your friend or family member about something interesting that happened to you recently. Remember to plan your answer and use paragraphs, just as you would in an essay.

How you sign off depends again on the person to whom you are writing. 'Love,' is probably the most common way to sign off. Other possibilities are, 'All the best,' 'Regards,' 'Thanks again,' or 'Best wishes,'.

QUESTION 1, SECTION 3, PAPER 1, JUNIOR CERT HL, 2011

*Read the letter on **Page 2** of **Paper X** written by the broadcaster, John Kelly, to his younger self. This letter is adapted from* With Love from me … to me. A Letter to my Sixteen-Year-Old Self *edited by Joseph Galliano.*

*Write **a letter** to your imaginary future son or daughter offering him or her advice on some significant milestones in his or her life. You might include such events as: first day at school, first disco, sitting the Junior Certificate examinations, etc.* (30 marks)

1. **Q** What **form** will my writing take?

   A This will be an informal letter.

2. **Q** What will be the **content** of the piece?

   A The question suggests some ideas you may wish to include in your answer. You are not bound by these suggestions, but they can be a useful starting point, particularly if you find it difficult to think of ideas. Whatever you decide to discuss in your letter, you must give advice. This is stipulated in the question.

3. **Q** Who will my **audience** be?

   A You are writing this letter to your future son or daughter.

4. **Q** What **register** will I use?

   A Your language should be reasonably chatty and informal. The level of formality is up to you, of course, but you are talking to a close family member. At the same time, you are a parent offering advice to a child, so your tone may well be serious in places.

Sample Informal Letter 1

25 Castle View,
Naas,
Co. Kildare.

When writing an informal letter do not include the receiver's address

14th September 2012

Dear Cormac,

I am sure that, just as I did at your age, you think you know it all. And maybe you do. But on the off-chance that you might take advice better than I did when I was young, I'm going to offer you some.

Chatty, informal tone

You are facing a life full of challenges and thrills. I wish I could spare you the bad bits, but I don't think that's possible. All I can do is tell you what I have learned along the way. Make of it what you will.

A significant milestone is discussed and advice is given on how to cope with it

First, I would like you to know that nothing is permanent. Good things might not last, but neither do bad things. For example, your first day at school might be terrible, but it will end in a few hours and you will never have to face it again. The scary teachers and unfamiliar classmates will become part of your everyday routine and they will not be scary or unfamiliar after the first week. Hang in there and things will get better.

You will make friends and lose friends as you grow older. You will keep the good friends. You will dress with care for your first school disco, but you may well come home disappointed. Life is not like the films. Love is not around every corner. And even if it is, it can end in heartbreak. Or it can end in happiness. That's the way life is. Nothing is certain.

You will study for exams, and if you are sensible you will study well in advance of the exam date. Although, if you are anything like me, you are already staring into space and saying 'Yeah, yeah,' as you read this. Do your best, but remember too that there *is more to life than exams. Always keep a balance between work and play.*

Above all, I want you to know that you should stick with the people and the things you care about. Everything else passes. Life is all about change. Embrace the good and learn from the bad. Know that your family and your friends are always there for you, so don't forget to turn to them if you ever need help. And most important, listen to your old dad!

With love,
Cian

Write a letter to your pen pal telling him or her about a good book you have enjoyed recently.
(Adapted from the Junior Certificate Examination 2003)

1. **Q** What **form** will my writing take?
   A This will be an informal letter.

2. **Q** What will be the **content** of the piece?
   A The letter will be a review of a book you have enjoyed. If you cannot think of a book you have read recently, you may use one of your set texts for this task.

3. **Q** Who will my **audience** be?
   A You will be writing to a pen pal: probably someone from a different country.

4. **Q** What **register** will I use?
   A Your language should be informal and chatty. When you are telling your pen pal about the book, you should be persuasive and descriptive.

Sample Informal Letter 2

22 Marian Park,

Ballyshannon,

Co. Donegal.

When writing an informal letter do not include the receiver's address

14th September 2012

Dear Marta,

How are you? It was great to get your last letter telling me all about your school and your family. It sounds like you're having a tough time revising for your summer tests.

Chatty, informal tone

If you are looking for something to distract you from all the study, I can recommend a book you might enjoy. It's The Diary of Anne Frank, *and it's a book everyone should read.*

Book review, as asked for in the question. Review is linked to letter by mention of shared interests

It's written by Anne Frank, a young Jewish girl living in Holland during World War Two. She and her family are forced to hide in an attic to avoid capture by the Nazis and her diary entries bring the incredible story to life. It's hard to believe that someone our own age had to stay hidden in such a small space for so long, in fear of her life. The book is, as its title suggests, a diary, and it gives us a window into Anne Frank's most personal thoughts and feelings. I won't tell you too much about the story in case you are planning to read it. You really should, it's the best book I have read in a long time and I think you'd love it too.

If you have read anything recently that you think I'd enjoy, let me know. I think we share a lot of the same tastes and I'd trust you to pick something interesting.

Well, I'd better sign off now. I can hear Mum calling me from upstairs, which probably means that she's seen the state of my bedroom. If she has, I'm in big trouble!

Write soon. I love catching up with all the news and hearing what you've been up to.

All the best,

Caoimhe

Informal sign-off

Question

You are on holidays with your family. Write the email you would send to a friend at home, describing your trip.

1. **Q** What **form** will my writing take?

   A This will be an email, which is similar to an informal letter in content and tone.

2. **Q** What will be the **content** of the piece?

   A You should give details of your holiday, as asked for in the question. Include some day-to-day activities and perhaps one or two highlights of the trip.

3. **Q** Who will my **audience** be?

   A The audience will be a friend of yours, so your writing will be relaxed.

4. **Q** What **register** will I use?

   A Your language should be chatty and informal, but you should not forget that you are writing a piece in an English exam. You may be unlikely to write to your friend in such a correct and tame way, but this is an exercise in language use. Some slang would be acceptable here, but try not to overdo it.

Sample Email

Hi Michael,

How are things? I just thought I'd send you a quick 'hello' from sunny Spain and make you jealous by telling you what we've been up to while you're stuck at home in the rain.

We're staying in a small resort by the sea about an hour's drive from Barcelona. Dad splashed out on a chalet with air conditioning this year, probably because of all the moaning last summer when we nearly baked alive in that tiny mobile home. I'm loving it here. This place has it all. There's even a bar in the middle of the main pool and you can swim up to it, buy an ice cream and eat it without even getting out of the water.

The beach is only a ten-minute walk from the hotel and Dad takes us there most afternoons. We rent pedal boats and head out past the swimmers and then we can jump off the boat and swim around in the deep water. I'd love to have a go on a jet ski but Mum won't hear of it. I might talk her around though. We'll see.

Even though we're spending most of our time in the pool or in the sea, we do go on some day trips. It was a bit cloudy on Tuesday, so we went up to Barcelona. Mum and Dad dragged us around churches and parks for ages, which was okay I suppose, but the best bit of the day was when we went to Camp Nou. It wasn't just a tour of the pitch; we got to go into the changing rooms and everything. They have life-sized cardboard cut-outs of the players and you can get your photo taken with them. I got one with Messi and Iniesta. It really looks like I'm standing between them. Wait until you see it. It's amazing.

Well, I'd better go now. I've already paid a euro for fifteen minutes on the internet. A postcard would have been cheaper.

See you when I get back the week after next,

Seán

There is no need to write your address when writing an email

Chatty, informal tone

Even though you may be writing to a friend, try to remember that this is an exam task. Don't use bad language, text language or symbols

You were asked to describe your holiday, so give some details of what you do every day, as well as any highlights of the holiday

Informal sign-off

INSTRUCTIONS

This task, which seems easy at first glance, requires you to be organised in your approach. Planning is essential. Remember, you are writing to inform.

If you have the choice, write a set of instructions for a game or task with which you are very familiar.

Think through each of the steps involved and make a quick plan. This need only be a word or two for each step of the instructions. By doing this, you will ensure that you tackle the points in the right order and that you do not leave anything out.

Give a brief statement outlining the aim of the game or the purpose of the instructions: 'The aim of Snap is to win the game by collecting all the cards from the other players.'

- If this set of instructions requires the reader to have any special equipment or ingredients, list these first.
- Use headings, numbers or bullet points.
- Keep your sentences short and clear.
- Don't use technical terms your reader may not understand. If you do have to use any technical terms, explain them clearly and concisely in a way that anyone could understand.
- You may wish to advise the reader how to avoid certain common pitfalls. For example, if you were writing a piece on travel, you might wish to say something like: 'Before you leave for the airport, weigh your bag on your bathroom scales. Check that it is under the weight allowed by your airline (usually 20kg) as if it exceeds this limit, you will be charged extra.'

Question

Choose one of your favourite games and, for the benefit of a person who does not know how to play it, explain the purpose and general rules of the game.

1. **Q** What **form** will my writing take?

   A This will be a set of instructions.

2. **Q** What will be the **content** of the piece?

   A The content will consist of the list of equipment, aim and rules of Snap.

3. **Q** Who will my **audience** be?

   A Children and adults read instructions for card games, so they should be easily understood by anyone aged ten or older.

4. **Q** What **register** will I use?

   A Your language should be impersonal and informative. Clarity (being clear) and brevity (being brief) are the keys here: you should not include anything that is not absolutely necessary.

Sample Answer 1

SNAP

The aim of Snap is to win the game by collecting all the cards from the other players.

If you are allowed to choose a game of your choice, it is a good idea to pick a very simple game

You will need

A deck of cards. This can be a standard deck or, if very young children are playing, a deck of picture cards. It does not matter, as long as there are matching pairs in the deck.

A second deck of cards may be needed if there are more than four players.

Try to keep your instructions consistent. Keep an eye on the tenses you use

Clarity (be clear) and brevity (keep your instructions as brief as possible) will get you a high grade in a task like this

Instructions

* *Two or more players sit opposite each other or in a circle around a table. They should be easily able to reach the centre of the table.*

- *All the cards are shuffled and dealt out to the players. The cards must be dealt face-down and the players may not look at their cards.*

- *If there are more than four players, a second deck may be used.*

- *Players stack their cards neatly if the dealer has not already done this.*

- *The player to the left of the dealer takes one of his/her cards and places it, face-up, in the centre of the table. He/she does not look at the card before doing this.*

- *The next player does the same, and so on around the circle of players.*

- *If two cards placed consecutively are of the same numeric value (regardless of suit) the player who sees the match first calls 'Snap' and places his/her hand on the pile. If several players call 'Snap' at the same time, the player whose hand reaches the pile first wins the turn.*

- *The player who wins the turn takes all the cards from the centre of the table, shuffles them, and places them face-down underneath his or her own stack of cards.*

- *Any player who runs out of cards is disqualified and must leave the game.*

Possible pitfalls addressed

- *A player who calls 'Snap' when there is no match must forfeit two of his or her cards to each of the other players.*

- *The winner is the player who ends up with all the cards.*

- *If the players mutually agree to end the game early, the winner is the player with the most cards.*

QUESTION 1, SECTION 3, PAPER 1, JUNIOR CERT HL, 2007

Look at the material adapted from the Irish Cancer Society's
*Sun Smart campaign that appears on **Page 2** of **Paper X***
(shown below).

Write a set of instructions – one for each picture – designed
to help people enjoy the summer sun safely.

Make sure to put the number of each picture beside the
instruction associated with it. (30 marks)

How to be Sun Smart

The sun produces ultraviolet radiation that is harmful to human skin and can lead to skin cancer. The good news is that taking a few simple measures can prevent much of this damage. Common sense would suggest protecting the skin from the sun, especially during those times of the day when the sun is hottest.

Picture **1**

Picture **2**

Picture **3**

Picture **4**

Picture **5**

Picture **6**

---

1. **Q** What **form** will my writing take?

   A This will be a set of six short instructions.

2. **Q** What will be the **content** of the piece?

   A There will be one instruction to accompany each picture.

   The pictures will dictate the content of each instruction.

3. **Q** Who will my **audience** be?

A People who are planning to spend time in the sun.

4. **Q** What **register** will I use?

A Your language should be informative and should include some brief explanations as to **why** people should do what you are suggesting. For example, you should not just tell people to wear a hat, but you should also tell them that wearing a hat will protect their neck, face and ears.

Sample Answer 2

As the question asked for one instruction per picture, you must structure your sentences in such a way that each sentence contains all the necessary information to accompany the picture

Your tone should encourage people to obey you. They have a choice and do not have to follow these instructions. You need to explain why they should

Picture 1: Stay in the shade to avoid the sun's harmful UV rays, particularly during the hottest times of the day.

Picture 2: Protect your skin by wearing a t-shirt or any other shirt with a close weave.

Picture 3: Protect your face, neck and ears by wearing a sun hat with a wide brim or a neck flap.

Picture 4: Before you go out in the sun, apply sun cream with a factor of 15 or higher and reapply it regularly throughout the day, particularly after swimming.

Picture 5: Protect your eyesight by wearing sunglasses which give protection against UV rays.

Picture 6: Avoid the sun completely or at least stay in the shade between 11 am and 3pm if possible, as the sun is at its hottest between those times.

QUESTION 2, SECTION 3, PAPER 1, JUNIOR CERT HL, 2007

Write a list of safety guidelines to be displayed on a poster ***EITHER*** *in your school's Science Lab* ***OR*** *in the Woodwork, Metalwork or Home Economics room.* (30 marks)

1. **Q** What **form** will my writing take?

   A This will be a set of numbered guidelines.

2. **Q** What will be the **content** of the piece?

   A The guidelines will consist of rules designed to keep students safe while in the lab.

3. **Q** Who will my **audience** be?

   A The audience will be secondary school students.

4. **Q** What **register** will I use?

   A Your language should be formal and impersonal.

As these are safety guidelines, you will not be suggesting to the students how they should behave: you will be telling them how they must behave. You do not have to explain yourself or justify your rules.

Sample Answer 3

- *Do not enter the laboratory without a teacher's permission.*

- *Long hair must be tied back, and all dangling jewellery removed before entering the laboratory.*

- *Lab coats must be worn at all times.*

- *Students must wear goggles and/or gloves when instructed to do so by a teacher and must not take them off until the teacher says it is safe to do so.*

- *Keep the aisles clear of bags, coats and any other personal items at all times.*

- *Only place books or other equipment on the desk if you are instructed to do so by a teacher.*

- *Do not touch any equipment, chemicals or other materials in the laboratory area unless you are instructed to do so by a teacher.*

The rules are listed in a sensible order. For example, students are told how they must dress before they are told how to safely complete an experiment

Instructions are clear and brief

- *Do not bring food or drink into the laboratory.*

Safety is number one here, so you should tell students what to do if something goes wrong

- *Do not taste anything in the laboratory. If any substance is accidentally taken into the mouth, the student must spit it out immediately, rinse out his or her mouth with water and then report the incident to a teacher.*

The instructions follow a logical order throughout

- *All cuts, burns or breakages of equipment must be reported to a teacher.*

- *Before using any chemical, the label on the bottle must be checked twice to ensure it is the correct chemical for that particular experiment.*

- *Do not overfill test tubes.*

- *When heating a test tube, ensure that the top of the tube is pointed away from yourself and any other students who are nearby.*

- *All equipment must be carefully cleaned and returned to its proper place in the laboratory.*

- *Wash your hands when you have finished your practical work.*

- *Behave in a responsible manner at all times.*

SPEECHES AND SHORT TALKS

You may be asked to write a short talk or a speech as part of the Functional Writing section or you may choose to write a speech in the Personal Writing section. Whichever is the case, the most important things to remember are:

a) your audience

b) planning your speech

If you are giving a talk, the tone and the form of address can be less formal than in a speech.

Imagine you are delivering the speech aloud. You want to capture your audience's attention and hold it. You don't want them to wonder what the speech was about or what point you were trying to make.

Before you even begin to plan your talk/speech, underline the key words in the question and decide the following:

1. Have I been asked to write a speech or a short talk?
2. Who is my target audience? Who will be listening to me?
3. What will my speech or talk be about? What point or points will I be trying to make?

Open with the correct form of address: 'Ladies and Gentlemen' or 'My fellow students', for example. You always begin by addressing the most important person in the room: 'Lord Mayor, my fellow students ...'

If you are giving a talk, the tone and the form of address can be less formal than in a speech.

Revise the section on 'Writing to argue, debate or make a case – Key Features' on page 16.

QUESTION 1, SECTION 3, PAPER 1, JUNIOR CERT HL, 2009

*You have been asked by the Principal of your school to speak to the students preparing to take their Junior Certificate examinations in June 2010. Based on your experience of preparing for your own Junior Certificate examinations, write the text of **the talk** you would give to the students, offering them guidance and encouragement.* (30 marks)

1. **Q** What **form** will my writing take?

   A This will be a short talk.

2. **Q** What will be the **content** of the piece?

   A The talk will give students both advice **and** encouragement. Personal anecdotes will be used to illustrate some of the points being made.

3. **Q** Who will my **audience** be?

   A The audience will be third-year students in your school.

4. **Q** What **register** will I use?

   A Your language should be quite chatty and relaxed. You should also try to persuade the students to take your advice.

Sample Talk

Informal opening is appropriate for a talk

Hello everybody. I can see that you're all wondering what on earth a transition year student is doing on stage at the third-year assembly, but there is a good reason. Mr McCarthy asked me to say a few words to you about the day you think will never come: the tenth of June next year. Yes, I know it seems a long way away now, but trust me, it will be upon you sooner than you think.

Rhetorical questions draw the listeners in and make them feel that the speaker is on their side

You have probably already been given a lot of advice and heard a lot about the exam from parents, teachers and even brothers and sisters. It's hard to take it all in, though, isn't it? I know I felt fed up when I was constantly being told to revise, to plan, to focus, to organise myself. It seemed that the nagging would never end. However, if I could go back in time and sit where you are sitting now, I'd listen a lot more carefully to everything I was told.

The one thing I would definitely do differently if I had my time over is be more organised. I found that some days I spent more time searching for notes and books than I spent studying. Or else I devoted myself to one subject at the expense of the others. I would strongly advise you all to make a study timetable and stick to it. Don't let things pile up until closer to the day of the exam. That never pays off. As Benjamin Franklin famously said, 'By failing to prepare, you are preparing to fail.'

The task specified 'advice' so it is important to give some solid, practical advice

It's not all doom and gloom, though, preparing for the Junior Cert. Yes, it is an important exam and yes, it is your first big state exam, but you will get through it. We all do. And don't forget that if your parents see that you are on top of your work from the start of the year, they will be far less likely to nag you and much more likely to let you go out with your friends at the weekend! That's one of the best reasons I can think of for sorting yourself out in September and not letting the work mount up.

The task also stated that students should be encouraged

Finally this morning, I'd just like to say that I'm sure you'll all do brilliantly in June. The best of luck to each and every one of you!

Definite conclusion

REPORTS

When you are writing a report, ask yourself the following questions:

1. Who has asked me to write the report and why?
2. What is the problem or issue on which I am reporting?
3. Do I need facts and figures?
4. What topics are to be covered?
5. What is supposed to happen as a result of the report?

Planning your report

- Give your report a title. This can be a simple rewording of the question.
- State the aim of the report in the introduction/title.
- Say who commissioned (asked you to write) the report and what was examined as a result.
- State what research was carried out.
- Look at the facts, detail any problems and highlight any good points.
- If you wish, you may use bullet points or numbers to organise your findings.
- Draw a conclusion from what you have just outlined.
- Make recommendations for remedying any problems.

QUESTION 1, **SECTION 3, PAPER 1, JUNIOR CERT HL, 2008**

You are a member of your school's Student Council. As there are now students from a range of different nationalities attending the school, your Principal has asked the Council to come up with some suggestions to help your school to develop as an intercultural community.

Write a report to be submitted by the Student Council to the Principal outlining your ideas. (30 marks)

1. **Q** What **form** will my writing take?
   A This will be a report with bullets and/or numbering.

2. **Q** What will be the **content** of the piece?
   A The report will outline practical ways in which students could become more aware of and supportive of the different cultures represented in the school.

3. **Q** Who will my **audience** be?
   A The audience will be the school principal.

4. **Q** What **register** will I use?

    A Your language should be formal, impersonal and precise.

Sample Report

Report on the ways in which the school could be developed as an intercultural community

Title/introduction

Terms of reference

This report was compiled by the Student Council and commissioned by Mr Eoghan Herlihy, Principal, St Columba's College, Ennis, to investigate the ways in which changes could be made to the school in order to reflect the different nationalities of the students attending the school. The report also includes recommendations based on the findings.

Who commissioned the report

Methods of gathering information

*A total of 150 students were given a detailed questionnaire designed to establish what they are dissatisfied with at present and what changes they would like to see brought about.
The staff were also questioned and asked if there were any suggestions they would make or whether they had ideas about ways in which classes could be tailored to help develop an awareness of the different nationalities in the school.*

Procedure

Findings

- *89 per cent of the students surveyed feel that the school needs to change to accommodate the growing number of students from other countries.*

Findings. Bullets and numbering are optional

- *94 per cent of students surveyed feel that they do not know much about the customs, language and culture of the other nationalities represented in the school and say they would like to know more.*

Language of information used throughout. No opinion given

- *The staff members who were interviewed all agreed that they would be happy to work with the Student Council in helping to teach students about other cultures.*

Conclusions

Based on the findings of this report, it would appear that the majority of staff and students are keen to see the school develop, and to embrace the different cultures which are now so widely represented in our community.

Recommendations

Suggestions/ recommendations

The art classes should make posters for the reception area of the school, welcoming visitors in each of the different languages of the different nationalities represented in the school.

On an agreed day each month, students should be allowed to use the cookery room to make foods from different countries. These could be put on tables in the assembly room and tasted at lunch time.

CSPE classes could give students from other countries the opportunity to talk to their fellow classmates about their countries of origin, and how they feel about living in Ireland.

Signed

Name of person who compiled report (optional)

Marie O'Sullivan

Chairperson
Student Council
17th September 2012

REVIEWS

When you are writing a review of a film, book, concert or television programme, remember to give your own opinion. Think about the content and decide what you are going to say about the quality.

Your review should be structured as follows:

Introduction
- Tell the reader what you are going to review.
- If it's a book, give the title and the name of the author.
- If it's a film, give the names of the principal actors and director.
- If it's a concert, give the name of the performer(s) and venue.

Description

Describe the film/book/CD/concert in some detail but remember not to give away the ending.

Evaluation

Tell the reader what you thought of the film, etc. Your opinion is important; it is what the reader wants to know. Explain why you liked or disliked it. Think of the advice you've been given for answering questions on Paper 2; a lot of it applies here. It is not enough to say that you found the film 'boring' or 'brilliant'; you must say why.

Think of your audience when you say what you liked and disliked about the film/book/event. Are you writing for your peers (school magazine) or a serious publication? Is this film or book in a series with which they are likely to be familiar? (For example James Bond, Twilight, Harry Potter.) You may wish to refer to previous books/films if that is the case, for example: 'This is the third book in the Twilight series and it came as somewhat of a disappointment to me.'

Recommendation

End with a recommendation in favour of the film/book if you liked it. If you didn't, advise your readers not to waste their time and money.

Film genres

There are several main genres of film with which you should be familiar, and each has a vocabulary generally associated with it. Listed below are some words and phrases which you might find helpful when writing a film review. Remember, some words and phrases can apply to several different genres, so feel free to mix and match.

Action/adventure

Big-budget
High-energy stunts
Natural disasters
'Good-guy' heroes
Audience escapism *(those watching can lose themselves in the imaginative world of the film)*
Non-stop action
Espionage (spying)

Comedy

Spoof *(a film which light-heartedly mocks something serious)*
Slapstick *(characterised by lots of physical action)*
Romantic comedy
Black humour *(a type of humour in which human suffering, and even death, is viewed as absurd)*
One-liners
Light-hearted plots
Exaggerated situations

Crime/gangster

Mobsters *(members of a criminal gang)*
Hoodlums *(thugs)*
Underworld figures
Sinister, ruthless villains
Double-crossing
Characters operate outside the law
Serial killer

Epic *(usually features heroic deeds, and is set during a war or over a long period of time)*
Mythic
Legendary
Hero
Spectacular
Sweeping musical score
Elaborate, lavish costumes

Musical
Song and dance routines
Full-scale scores
Choreography
Extravaganza
Showcases the talent of ...

Sci-fi/science fiction
Quests
Futuristic
Special effects
Technology
Alien life
Malevolent *(wishing harm to others)*
Destroy humankind
Peril
The unknown

War
Combat
Violence
Heartbreak
Horror
Human interest stories
Condemns war
Inhumanity
Gory
Over-the-top fight scenes
Battlefield
Poignant *(deeply moving or touching)*

Question

Write a review for a young people's magazine of any book, film, computer game or concert you have recently experienced.

Your answer should include an introduction, description, evaluation and recommendation.

1. **Q** What **form** will my writing take?

   A This will be a review. (The option selected for the purpose of this sample answer is a film.)

2. **Q** What will be the **content** of the piece?

   A You will have to include all the elements mentioned in the question: introduction, description, evaluation and recommendation. Your own opinion will be shown clearly throughout the review.

3. **Q** Who will my **audience** be?

   A The audience will be young people around the same age as yourself.

4. **Q** What **register** will I use?

   A Your language should be chatty and relaxed. The section which outlines the film plot should be narrative.

Sample Review 1

Movie: War Horse

Introduction mentions director and name of film

Steven Spielberg's superb epic War Horse *opened at cinemas nationwide this weekend and, in the interests of keeping our readers informed, I rushed off to see it.*

War Horse *is an adaptation of Michael Morpugo's novel of the same name. Having read and greatly enjoyed the book several years ago, I was naturally interested to see if the film would manage to capture all the excitement and all the sentiment that kept me* glued to the novel from start to finish. I wasn't disappointed. This film was a delight, and it more than lived up to my expectations.

Tone is positive

The story begins in a beautiful village in England, where tenant farmer Ted Narracott (Peter Mullan) buys a magnificent young horse called Joey. Ted originally intended to buy a plough horse to work on his farm and has to face his wife's wrath when he brings home the unsuitable, unbroken colt. Ted's son Albert (Jeremy Irvine) falls for Joey and promises his mother (Emily Watson) that he will train him to pull the plough. He succeeds against all the odds and it looks as if his family's harvest and rent for the coming year are safe. But disaster strikes and a storm wipes out their entire crop. The family's debts threaten to cripple them and, as war breaks out in Europe, Ted decides to raise the money he needs by selling Joey to the army.

Description, giving enough detail to let the readers judge whether or not it's the sort of story that might interest them, but the ending is not given away

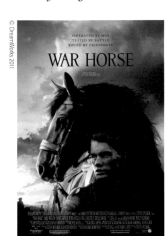

© DreamWorks 2011

Albert is heartbroken but the cavalry captain who buys Joey promises to return him after the war, if he can. His promise comes to nothing, sadly, and he is killed in action. Joey is captured by the Germans and then, in a series of heart-wrenching plot twists, comes under the care of a French farmer and his granddaughter. His peaceful time on the farm is short-lived and soon Joey is back at the front, struggling to stay alive in appalling conditions. I won't give too much away but suffice to say that Joey and Albert meet again, both fighting for their lives. Will there be a happy ending for the two brave heroes? Well, you'll have to go and see the film if you want to find out.

War Horse is the perfect choice for a family evening at the cinema. There is virtually no let-up in the drama from start to finish. I was on the edge of my seat for most of it, and I already knew how the story ended.

Mentions those to whom the film might appeal

The film is rated 12A but I think it could equally easily be rated PG. While there are plenty of war scenes, they are not particularly

Evaluation – the writer gives opinions and explains them

gruesome, and neither the humans' nor the horses' suffering is graphically shown.

This is a must-see film. It's long: nearly two and a half hours, but the characters are so engaging and the story so gripping that you won't notice the time fly by. Trot on down to your local cinema this weekend and watch War Horse. *You won't regret it.*

Sample Review 2

Computer Game – Star Wars: The Old Republic

It is always a good idea to mention if the game is a sequel to another game. This helps the reader to place the game in context

This multi-player, online role-playing game is a sequel to the hugely successful Knights of the Old Republic. *Those who enjoyed the last game will be happy to recognise some familiar faces in this outstanding new release.*

© BioWare, LucasArts 2011

Set several hundred years after the events in Knights of the Old Republic *(and featuring some familiar faces),* Star Wars: The Old Republic *(generally abbreviated to SWTOR) puts players in the middle of a gigantic war between the Empire and the Republic.*

Rhetorical questions draw the reader in

Do you fancy yourself as a Sith, a Jedi or another classic Star Wars character in this epic struggle? The choice is yours. Players can be whoever they want and can decide to support the light or the dark side of the Force. Along the way, players can choose to befriend comrades who will help or possibly betray them as they battle their enemies.

Someone reading this type of review is likely to be familiar with the terms/ characters

This is a superb, fast-paced game which more than lives up to the high standard set by its predecessor. It's no surprise that, within three days of its release, it had more than one million subscribers. SWTOR can only be fully appreciated once you throw yourself into it and lose yourself in your online character. Then, and only then, will you understand its popularity. The light-sabre duels alone are enough to win over even the most ardent World of Warcraft *fan.*

Recommendation *Try this game. You won't regret it.*

DVD and book blurbs

You may also be asked to write a blurb for the back of a DVD cover, for example. This is a **shorter** task than a review for a magazine or a newspaper, but there are similarities. The main difference between a review and a blurb is that the blurb must always be positive. You want to write it in such a way that the person who picks up the book or the DVD will be intrigued and enticed and want to buy the item. A blurb is like a cross between an advertisement and a review.

The length of the blurb may not be specified, but as a general rule you should not exceed 150 words or fifteen lines of your answer booklet. Remember, this is a rough guide. You do not need to count the number of words you have written, but you should be aware that the average number of words to the line is ten.

This task is similar to an advertisement in that it will test your ability to write **briefly** but **persuasively**. This can be more difficult than it might appear. If you are thinking of attempting a blurb on the day of the exam, you should definitely have had plenty of practice writing them beforehand. Read the blurbs on the back of your DVD covers and books at home to give yourself some inspiration.

QUESTION 2, SECTION 3, PAPER 1, JUNIOR CERT HL, 2006

Most books and DVDs have a short blurb on the outside of the back cover. Typically this is a brief text which describes and praises the plot, characterisation, acting, etc. Write such a blurb for any book or DVD of your choice. (30 marks)

1. **Q** What **form** will my writing take?

   A This will be a short blurb.

2. **Q** What will be the **content** of the piece?

   A You will have to give a brief description of the plot of the film or book, plus any relevant information about actors, directors, etc.

3. **Q** Who will my **audience** be?

   A The audience will be the general public.

4. **Q** What **register** will I use?

   A Your language should be persuasive, descriptive and enthusiastic. In as short a space as possible, you should convince people to buy the DVD or the book.

Sample Blurb

Pompeii by Robert Harris

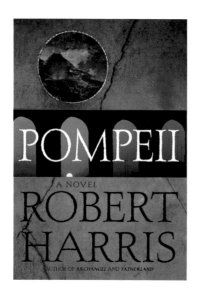

It's August in Italy. The heat has driven Rome's wealthiest citizens to their summer villas in Pompeii. But their water supply is dwindling. The mighty aquaduct, the Aqua Augusta, has dried to a trickle and, without water, life in the towns on the Bay of Naples is under threat.

It's up to the young engineer Attilius to save the day. But Ampliatus, a corrupt millionaire, seems bent on stopping Attilius finding the source of the water failure. Why? Ampliatus' beautiful daughter is determined to thwart her father's murderous plans and to help Attilius. What none of them realises, however, is that time is running out. Mount Vesuvius is about to blow, with unimaginable force. Who will survive one of the most destructive forces ever unleashed by nature?

Robert Harris' explosive blockbuster brings to life the thrilling story of the most famous volcanic eruption in history.

NEWS REPORTS AND ARTICLES

When you are writing an article, you should include:

- **Headline, byline** and **subheading**.

The **headline** is the title. It should be clear and maybe even amusing, depending on the topic and the publication for which you are writing. For example, in a light-hearted article, the title might be snappy or humorous, using alliteration or a play on words.

The **byline** is the name of the person who has written the article. It is placed under the headline.

The **subheading** will give more details about the information contained in the headline. For example, the headline might read 'Gardaí seek missing man', while the subheading might read 'Galway father of three has not been seen since Thursday night'. An article may contain several subheadings, each breaking the text into sections. This is more common in tabloids than broadsheets.

Decide on the type of publication for which you are writing. This will determine the tone of your article and the type of language you use. If you are writing for a magazine, you may decide to use a more light-hearted approach than if you are writing for a serious broadsheet.

Think about the type of language you should use. If you are writing a serious article about a controversial topic, you will want to make a case supported with facts and figures where possible. Your writing will be quite formal. If you are writing a more light-hearted article on a less serious topic, you may wish to write less formally and you may decide to include several personal anecdotes (funny little stories from your own experiences).

Read as many articles as you can between now and the exam. Most of the major newspapers are available online, so you don't even need to buy a paper to keep up with the news.

There are two main types of article:

News report

When you are planning a news story, think of an inverted (upside down) pyramid. The most important information is at the top (beginning of article) and the least important information is at the bottom (end of article). This way, the article will still make sense even if it is severely edited due to space restrictions.

Unless you are writing a news article for a tabloid paper, your piece should not be opinionated.

- # Lead/Headline
- ## Who? What? Where? When? Why?
- **Detail 1. Detail 2. Detail 3.**
- **Final Detail**

Feature article

A feature article is usually intended to amuse or inform. It often centres on human interest stories and can be opinionated. Personal anecdotes may be used and the tone is frequently light-hearted. Of course, the topic may be a serious one, in which case the tone should be adjusted accordingly. Read the question carefully and if it is linked to the Reading section, for example, study the text on which it is based. This will give you a clear idea of what is required.

Sample News Article

Headline   ***GARDAÍ THREATENED BY ARMED MAN***

Byline   *Mark O'Connor*

Main fact   *Gardaí are investigating an incident in which two members of the force were threatened with a firearm when they arrived to break up a fight outside a pub in Co. Clare late on Thursday night.*

Facts become less important to main body of article as we read on. The piece could be cut and it would still make sense   *The disturbance occurred in Ennis town and is believed to have been started by two local men who have been involved in feuds for the past five years.*

Gardaí responded to a call from the owner of the public house and as they arrived on the scene at about 11.30 pm, a man produced a .38 revolver and pointed it at them.

Superintendent Michael Barry is leading the investigation into the altercation. He says that the men in question discarded the firearm and fled the scene on foot. They were pursued by the gardaí and were arrested a short distance from the town centre. The area was sealed off and witnesses were interviewed. The two men, who have been named locally as Dwayne Geasley (21) from Woodgrove Gardens in the town and Liam Dennehy (19), also from the town, were taken to Ennis Garda station. A file has been sent to the Director of Public Prosecutions.

In a follow-up search of two houses in the town, a number of weapons and two stolen cars were recovered. A man in his twenties was taken from one of the properties and brought to Ennis Garda station where he is helping gardaí with their enquiries.

Pub owner, Shane Moriarty, said that the incident was totally out of character for the area. 'This is a lovely, quiet spot,' he said. *Quotes from witness* 'The pub has been in my family for fifty years and in all that time nothing like this has ever happened. I don't know the men who were arrested. One of them came in for a drink and it seems the other fellow was waiting for him outside when he left. I heard shouting and sounds of fighting, so I called the guards immediately.' *The writer does not express any opinion on the story*

Ennis gardaí are appealing for witnesses to the incident.

QUESTION 2, SECTION 3, PAPER 1, JUNIOR CERT HL, 2005

Look at the Food Pyramid that appears on Page 4 of Paper X (shown overleaf). The recommended servings on the right state the fundamentals of a healthy diet.

Using the information provided, write a short article for your school magazine promoting healthy eating. (30 marks)

1. **Q** What **form** will my writing take?
   A This will be a feature article.

2. **Q** What will be the **content** of the piece?

   A The food pyramid gives basic guidelines about recommended servings of various foodstuffs. You need not stick to it rigidly but it can provide the basis of your article.

3. **Q** Who will my **audience** be?

   A The audience will be your fellow students.

4. **Q** What **register** will I use?

   A Your language should be persuasive and positive.

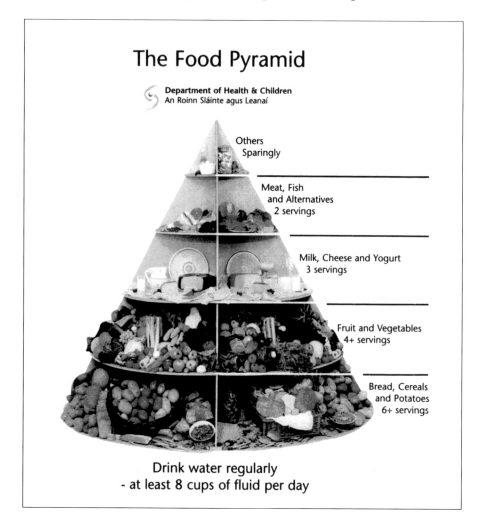

Sample Answer

NEW HABITS, NEW YOU

Niamh McCarthy

Simple steps to a happier, healthier lifestyle

We all know we should eat healthily. We've been told this by our parents for as long as we can remember; we're told this in school, and we're told this by the media. Yet we choose to ignore the advice, by and large. Well, maybe it's time we started listening and stopped snacking.

If we eat healthily, we'll look better, feel better, and have more money to spend on the things we really want. Not only do processed, sugary foods do our skin and hair no favours, but they are ridiculously expensive compared to the healthier options of fruit or a sandwich. One trip to the shop to buy crisps, cola and chocolate can easily set you back five euro. If you do that five or six times a week, you're potentially wasting a huge amount of money. Just think. If you saved that money up for twelve weeks or so, you could buy a laptop or an iPhone. That sounds much more tempting than that daily bag of pick 'n' mix, doesn't it?

So, now that we've looked at some of the reasons not to eat unhealthy food, it's time to look at ways to make it easier to eat healthily.

One of the first things you should do every day is to make sure you eat a good breakfast. Bread and cereals provide plenty of slow-release energy and will ensure you don't get the craving for tuck shop Mars bars at ten thirty. Fruit is a great way of getting natural sugars at breakfast time. Try a smoothie or even a glass of juice instead of a cup of tea with your cereal and toast.

It might be a good idea to make your school lunch before you make your filling breakfast. It's difficult to imagine you'll be hungry again after a bowl of porridge, a smoothie and a couple of slices of hot buttered toast. When you are making your lunch, try

Headline

Byline

Subheading

Use of 'We' makes the article more personal and less like a lecture

There is balance in the sentence: 'started listening and stopped snacking'

Money and appearance are important to many teens. These points show an awareness of the audience

Rhetorical questions appropriate for persuasive writing. This article is to promote healthy eating, which means persuading the readers to take your advice

Paragraphs are linked and are not just a series of disconnected points

Practical, positive advice

to avoid biscuits and bars. A sandwich, a fruit yoghurt and some cheese make up a nutritious lunch.

Brief conclusion, referring back to opening paragraphs

It is said that it takes three weeks to break a habit. That is not a lot of time. So try a healthy eating regime for three weeks. If, at the end of that time, you don't look better, have more energy and more money, and wonder why you ever craved junk food, I'll eat my hat!

COMPETITION ENTRIES

The form a competition entry should take is usually dictated by the person or organisation setting the rules and regulations.

Read the question carefully. Is there a word limit? Ask yourself how many lines of your answer book this would take up, assuming an average of ten words to the line.

Does the question tell you how the entry should be laid out? If not, you are free to choose a layout that suits you best. In general, however, it is probably best to stick to a simple layout: one or two paragraphs outlining the reasons why you should be chosen.

Does the question tell you what the content of the entry should be? Check and double check the wording of the question.

How many parts are there to the question? Is the word 'and' used in the question? Remember, this may mean there are two or more topics that you will need to cover in your answer.

You are trying to persuade the person judging the competition that you are the best choice. Bear this in mind when selecting your register. Use plenty of strong adjectives and adverbs when appropriate. Don't use qualifiers such as 'quite' and 'fairly'. These will weaken your case. Would you give a place on a space mission to someone who said that they were 'quite good at science' or 'fairly okay with heights'?

QUESTION 2, SECTION 3, PAPER 1, JUNIOR CERT HL, 2008

NASA (National Aeronautics and Space Administration) is running an international competition to send one student from Ireland on the next moon mission. You wish to enter the competition.

The following are the competition entry requirements:

1. *Entries should be between 170 and 200 words*
2. *You should outline*
   - *Your suitability for the mission*
   - *Why you wish to participate in the mission*

Complete your competition entry. (30 marks)

---

1. **Q** What **form** will my writing take?

   A There is no definite format expected for a competition entry, but you must be aware of the restrictions on the length of the piece. There is no need to count the words. Instead, you should have a rough idea of how many words to the line you write on average and multiply that by the number of lines you are using in the answer book. So, if you average ten words to the line, you will want to use up no more than about two-thirds (twenty lines or so) of the answer book page. The examiner will be experienced enough to judge at a glance if your piece is much too long or too short, so don't worry about the exact number of words. It is only a guideline.

2. **Q** What will be the **content** of the piece?

   A You must address both parts of the task. In other words, outline both your suitability for the mission and your reasons for wanting to participate. The two sections need not be dealt with in the same amount of detail, but it would be a good idea to think in terms of writing one short paragraph for each aspect.

3. **Q** Who will my **audience** be?

   A The audience will be adults whose job it is to pick the winning entry.

4. **Q** What **register** will I use?

   A Your language should be persuasive and enthusiastic.

Sample Answer

A rhetorical question can be a good way to draw the reader in and make them want to read on

Why on earth should you send an Irish student into space? And why me in particular? Well, I believe I am the right choice. I am a keen science student and I was the leader of the winning team at this year's prestigious 'Young Scientist' competition. Our project, 'Reaching Out to the Stars', looked at the possibility of colonising other planets. I believe our success proves that I work well with others and that I have plenty of initiative.

Scientific experiences are linked to this mission

I have always dreamt of going into space and the 'Young Scientist' project only fuelled that desire. Ireland does not have a space programme, but we have many potential space travellers and scientists: students who would be a positive asset to NASA in years to come. I believe that my participation in this mission

Having mentioned your suitability for the mission, you must also say why you wish to go

would generate huge Irish interest in NASA and in the study of science. I would love the chance to come back and tell other students what space travel is really like, and why they too should pursue their dreams of working with NASA some day. My dream is to reach out, not just to space, but also to future generations of scientists.

ADVERTISEMENTS

- An advertisement is meant to grab the reader's attention immediately.
- Decide what type of customer you are trying to attract. This will dictate the tone of your advertisement.
- Start with a strong headline if possible, making a bold statement and arousing curiosity.
- You may wish to ask a provocative question: 'Have you had enough of boring TV programmes?'
- Introduce your product in an appealing way.
- You may, if you wish, use bullet points to list the attractive features you have on offer.
- Elaborate on these points in the next part of your advertisement. Explain the benefits of these features in more detail.
- Be clear and be positive. Do not use negative words as they tend to put people off. Instead of saying, 'Don't delay!' you should say, 'Hurry!'
- Use plenty of adjectives.
- Make sure your grammar and spelling are correct.
- An advertisement may well be shorter than some of the other writing tasks but that does not mean it is the easiest option. In an advertisement, each word must work for you. Your job is to capture and hold your jaded readers' attention. People skip over ads in magazines and newspapers: how will you make yours stand out?

Sample Advertisement from a 'Discover Ireland' Campaign

Discover Ireland.ie

Sense of immediacy added by the words 'Right Here, Right Now'

Right Here, Right Now
Take Your Pick from Thrilling Water Sports
to High Culture

Mentions variety, appeals to many different types of tourist

Ireland's got a lot up its sleeve when it comes to things to do! Did you know that we're now one of Europe's top destinations for whale watching, or that surfing dudes flock to our beaches to catch sky-high waves, or that you can clip-clop along country roads in your own horse-drawn caravan?

Rhetorical questions, one of the features of persuasive writing. These draw the reader in

If you don't like getting intimate with the great outdoors, you can occupy yourself with a diverse range of sightseeing attractions from ancient monuments to multimedia interpretative centres, top theatres and art galleries and some of the most memorable festivals around the world!

Something for everyone; positive, upbeat tone. Lists more available options – short and to the point

And if you are looking for a special gift, take a look at our Irish Crafts Section for details of shops, galleries and studios recommended by the Crafts Council of Ireland.

Makes visiting Ireland sound fun

It's all on your doorstep, so what are you waiting for? There's more to life than work, so let's play!

Challenges reader to discover it for themselves

DESCRIBING A PICTURE

While this option may seem off-putting at first, it is actually quite easy once you know how to approach it.

- The purpose of this task is to test your ability to describe a picture as accurately as you possibly can.
- You will be writing an informative piece and you must avoid giving your own opinion. Be objective.
- Begin with an overall description and then move on to describing more of the details.
- Focus on the main aspects of the picture and then describe the less important details.
- Use plenty of adjectives.

Try to use the following terms:

- Background
- Foreground – the part of the picture which is nearest to the viewer
- Frame – the borders of the picture
- Left, right, centre, top, etc.
- Black and white/full colour/monochrome (varying shades of the same colour)

Imagine you are describing the picture over the phone. The person on the other end of the line is an artist who will draw a picture based on your description. Have you given them all the information they need?

EXAM **FOCUS**

Sample Description of a Photograph

Overall description is given. The girl is the focus of the picture, so she is described first

This black-and-white photograph shows a girl running down the right-hand footpath of a snow-covered city street. The girl is in the centre of the picture but has her back to the viewer. She is wearing a short, heavy winter coat which is flapping as she runs. The girl's right hand is holding her beret-style hat on her head, presumably to keep it from being blown off by the strong wind. The strength of the wind can be seen by the fact that the snow is falling in an almost horizontal direction. The girl is wearing heavy, dark tights and calf-length, light-coloured, flat-heeled boots. Her right leg is raised as the camera catches her in mid-stride.

Adjectives are used but there is no subjectivity

The street is wide, as is the footpath. There is a row of tall streetlights on the edge of the footpath. There are large tubs between the streetlights, each tub containing a small tree or shrub. There are no leaves on the plants; only bare branches can be seen.

To the left of the photograph is a tall building which runs from the left-hand frame as far as the centre of the photograph, where it disappears into the dense white of the snow-filled distance. It appears to be a commercial building with regularly spaced tall windows going to the top of the frame of the picture. The entrance to the building is half-way down the street and it juts out into the footpath. This entrance is covered by a square canopy.

There is no need to worry about writing a conclusion to a description of a picture

The top right-hand corner of the photograph is filled by a canopy. The building to which the canopy belongs is not visible in this shot. Icicles hang from the canopy and appear to be pointing in the direction of the running girl.

MEDIA STUDIES

The Media Studies section of Paper 1 is worth **40 marks**.
You should spend about **35 minutes** on this section.

Total: 40

You should be able to discuss various aspects of the media, including:

- Advertising
- Newspapers and magazines
- Television and radio
- Cartoons and comic strips

When you are analysing or discussing sections of the media, you must use the appropriate vocabulary. The terminology you will need is discussed in each section of this chapter.

As in the Functional Writing section, you must be aware of the audience and the register which is appropriate for each method of communication.

Remember, this is the section of the exam for which you have done the most preparation, even if you don't know it. Think for a minute about how long you spend each day on the internet, watching television, listening to the radio in the car, reading magazines or flicking through newspapers for sports reports. It is unlikely that you spend that much time revising for any other aspect of your course. All you need to do now is to put what you know into words.

ADVERTISING

Advertisements are designed to catch our attention, give us some information about a product and persuade us to buy that product. Sometimes we can even be persuaded to advertise products ourselves. Think of the brand names and logos on clothes, phones, computers, bags ... The list goes on.

Lifestyles

Advertisements can imply that purchasing a particular product or service will lead to an improvement in the purchaser's life. They sell the dream of ideal lifestyles featuring happy families, romance, luxury, glamour, success and physical attractiveness.

Language of advertising

The written text of an advertisement is called the **copy**. Various techniques are used to make the copy capture the interest of the target audience.

Advertisements are designed to persuade and inform. They can also try to create a sense of urgency by suggesting that this offer is for a limited time only, or that the product is so popular that it may well be sold out if you do not rush to buy it right now.

What type of aspirational lifestyle is portrayed in this magazine advertisement?

The verbs used are often imperative: 'hurry', 'go', 'rush', 'buy'. Punctuation marks – exclamation marks in particular – can add a sense of urgency and excitement. 'Hurry!' 'Not to be missed!'

Rhetorical questions engage the target audience: 'What are you waiting for?'

Buzz words are words or phrases which are used to make the product sound more appealing. Buzz words like 'revolutionary', 'latest', 'miracle' and so on have become so commonly used that they are almost clichés and have lost much of their impact.

Technical or scientific jargon is used to persuade the audience that the product is better than its rivals. Much of this jargon is meaningless but because it sounds scientific, consumers are often impressed and are willing to spend more money on the product than they might otherwise do. In advertisements for skincare products, for example, buzz words like 'pro-collagen', 'cellular' and 'regeneration' abound. Although they mean very little when examined individually, the overall impression created by such words is one of youth, science and beauty.

Slogans such as *'Always Coca-Cola'* or Nike's *'Just do it'* help to make the product memorable. Such slogans can remain the same for many years.

Alliteration, assonance, similes, personification, rhymes and so forth may be used. These make it easier to remember the slogan or catchphrase associated with the product. The car manufacturer Jaguar uses a number of these techniques in its various advertising campaigns. Look at the following examples.

- Don't dream it. Drive it! (**Alliteration**)
- Grace, space, pace (**Rhyme**)
- Unleash a Jaguar (**Personification: a jaguar is a large, wild cat**)
- Born to perform (**Assonance and personification**)

Humour is a common way of attracting the audience's attention. Puns are frequently used for comic effect.

New words may be coined, often using a combination of existing words: 'snacktivity', 'fruitilicious'.

Visuals

Pictures are a quick way to capture the audience's attention. The images used are often associated with a certain lifestyle or idea. Beautiful women, cute children or famous celebrities are commonly used to attract the audience. The images can be altered or Photoshopped to give an impression of perfection. When a celebrity is used to advertise a product, this is called **endorsement**.

The colours used are associated with certain moods or feelings.

Red: action, vitality, danger, passion, love, strength

Pink: love, femininity, romance

Green: nature, cleanliness

Gold: prestige, luxury, wealth

Silver: science, modernity, luxury

Yellow: joy, happiness, energy, warmth

Blue: tranquillity, health, cleanliness

White: innocence, purity, goodness

Orange: happiness, stimulation, creativity

Black: power, death, elegance, formality

What do you think the mood colour in this billboard is saying? Is it successful?

The people in the image may represent certain classes in society. They may be students, business people or parents. There may be gender stereotyping: a mother washing the dishes or a father mowing the lawn or fixing a car.

The typeface or font suits the image the advertisers want to get across.

Analysing an advertisement

This is one of the most common questions in the Junior Certificate exam. Ask yourself a few simple questions when approaching this type of question:

1. What is being advertised?
2. Can you identify the target audience? What sort of person do you think the ad is aimed at?
3. What benefits of the product or service are highlighted?
4. What do the visuals tell you?
5. What does the copy tell you?

You should refer back to the Functional Writing chapter of this book (page 109) for instructions on how to write an advertisement.

NEWSPAPERS

You should refer back to the Functional Writing section of this book (page 101) for instructions on how to write news articles and feature articles and to see an example of each type.

Types of newspaper and the differences between them

TABLOID

Small, A3 size pages

Informal language and slang

Simple language

Sensationalist headlines often using puns and alliteration

Lots of images

Generalisations

More human interest stories and celebrity gossip, including paparazzi photographs

One story usually dominates the front page and is accompanied by a large image

PARTS OF A NEWSPAPER

News reports

This is generally the first section in the paper and it includes factual reports of international and national news. Refer back to the section on news reports in the Functional Writing chapter (page 101) for more information and a sample article.

BROADSHEET

Large, A2 size pages

Formal language

More complex language

Informative headlines

Far more text than images

Statistics and facts given

News stories about politics and world affairs

Several stories on the front page

Editorial/opinion columns

This is the section of the newspaper where journalists and guest writers give their opinions on political or social issues.

Feature articles

These cover a wide variety of topics from celebrity gossip to informative pieces about lifestyles, gardening or health, for example. Refer back to the Functional Writing chapter (page 105) for more information and a sample feature article.

Sports reports

Reports and analysis of recent sports events.

Business section

This deals with financial matters.

Letters to the editor

Refer to the Functional Writing chapter (page 67) for more information and sample letters to the editor.

Entertainment section

This may include reviews of films and books, radio and television schedules and so forth.

Classified section

Advertising is one of the main sources of income for newspapers and most of the classified section is given over to advertisements. These are usually quite short. This section may also contain legal notices and notices about births, marriages and deaths.

MAGAZINES

Magazines are aimed at a particular target audience. If you look at the magazine section in any newsagent, you will see that there is something for almost everyone. Whether you are interested in fashion, gardening, computers, animals, fishing or just about anything else you can think of, there is a magazine for you.

The main purpose of most magazines is to entertain, although many also contain a large amount of information.

The language in the magazine reflects the target audience. A magazine aimed at young teenagers, for example, will use a lot of slang and very little complex language.

Like newspapers, magazines rely on advertising for a large part of their income. The advertisements reflect the content of the magazine. A magazine aimed at teenage girls will contain lots of advertisements for make-up and other beauty items.

Magazines, like newspapers, contain a number of different sections. These might include editorials, feature articles, letters to the editor, reviews, interviews and reports. The emphasis will be on opinion pieces.

RADIO AND TELEVISION

National radio stations

- These are funded by the government and by income generated from advertising.
- They broadcast nationwide.
- They broadcast twenty-four hours a day.
- Different stations offer different types of programme. RTÉ Radio One is a talk-based station which provides coverage of international and national news and sporting events, as well as chat shows and documentaries.
- The presenters of the programmes on national radio are usually well known and have a loyal following. The more popular the presenter, the more he or she is paid. Rival radio stations may try to hire popular presenters or DJs to raise the profile of their own station.

Local radio stations

- Some local stations may receive funding from the government but most rely on advertising for most of their income.
- They cover news and sporting events from their own locality.
- The majority of local radio stations do not broadcast twenty-four hours a day but are instead limited to peak times.
- Presenters of local radio programmes can be well known in their own locality, but as a rule they do not earn as much as presenters of national radio programmes.

Television

In the early days of television, stations tried to appeal to as wide an audience as possible. There were fewer channels and these covered everything from news to sporting events to music and chat shows. This type of television is called broadcasting, because it is aimed at a broad spectrum of the population. As time went on, more and more television stations began to appear and some of these aimed their programming at a specific **demographic** (section of the population). For example, certain channels covered nothing but sporting events or music or nature documentaries. This type of television is called narrowcasting, because it is aimed at a limited section of the population. It is a similar idea to specialised magazines which target a specific group and cover one subject only.

Television stations receive their funding in two ways. They may be funded wholly, or in part, by the government and licence fees or they may rely on advertising for some or all of their income.

When a television station relies on advertising for most of its income, its programming is restricted to a certain extent because advertisers can dictate – or at least influence – the sorts of programme they want shown. Advertisers prize programmes which attract the highest number of viewers and will pay more for time slots during these programmes. Therefore, programmes which are educational, for example, may not be shown on purely commercial channels as they are unlikely to draw as many viewers as soap operas or comedies. Television stations like the BBC do not get money from advertising, so are free to make and show the types of programme they want. They aim to serve the public interest and do not wish their independence to be compromised by having to answer to advertisers.

TV plays an important role in providing news

Advantages of television
- It can be educational. There are documentary channels devoted to history, nature and science, for example.
- It can bring you the latest news faster than the print media can.
- It is easier to understand certain things when they are explained using sound, images and movement. A film of a

volcano erupting is far more powerful than a description of such an eruption on the radio could hope to be.

- Television has entertainment value.

Disadvantages of television

- Watching television is a passive experience. The viewer has no control over the images being presented and the images are constantly changing, which means that there is little or no time to stop and think about what is being shown.

- Advertising plays such a large role in television programmes that it can make people overly materialistic and can create a consumer society in which we believe we need certain things to make us happy.

- People who spend too much time sitting and watching television can become unhealthy.

- Television watching is quite addictive and people who become 'hooked' on certain shows can find it difficult to give them up or do anything else when those shows are on.

- Children and young people are strongly influenced by the lifestyles and values they see promoted in television programmes. The nine o'clock watershed (a watershed is a dividing line) is an attempt by television stations to restrict the broadcasting times of adult programmes which may be unsuitable for younger audiences. However, now that television programmes can be recorded, such limits do not have the effect they had in the days when the only option was to watch programmes at the time they were broadcast. Also, many programmes can be watched on the internet, so it is very difficult to prevent young people watching adult programmes and films.

CARTOONS

The purpose of cartoons in the media may be simply to amuse or to make a satirical comment on a political or social issue. Satire is the ridicule of others – usually public figures – for behaviour that is considered foolish.

The cartoonist may draw caricatures of the person being satirised. Although the satirical cartoon may make us laugh, there is a serious purpose behind it.

Newspapers can also contain regular comic strips or cartoons whose purpose is purely to entertain us.

The work of two of Ireland's leading cartoonists …

Niall O'Loughlin

"What? You expect me to write on a *piece of paper?*"

Aongus Collins

SECTION 4, PAPER 1, JUNIOR CERT HL, 2007

Martyn Turner's cartoon below shows aliens viewing planet Earth in the future. Examine the cartoon and

(a) *State briefly what you think the cartoonist's message is.*
(20 marks)

(b) *Imagine that one of the aliens in the cartoon is a journalist. Write a brief article that he/she/it might write for the front page of* The Martian Times *on his/her/its return.* (20 marks)

Note: *The Stern Report mentioned in the cartoon refers to a recent report by economist Sir Nicholas Stern on the effect of human activity such as global warming on the world's climate.*

Sample Answer A

Although you are asked to state your opinion 'briefly', this question is worth twenty marks, so a certain amount of explanation is required. You should look at both the visual and the verbal elements of the cartoon.

This is the main point of the answer

The message in this satirical cartoon is a bleak one: take care of the planet or die with it.

The visual element of this cartoon is most striking. The

background is almost entirely black, which creates a gloomy and depressing atmosphere. Instead of twinkling stars, we see various pieces of refuse floating through space. Along with all of this debris is a copy of the Stern Report on the effects of climate change. The fact that this report is floating around in space with all the other rubbish suggests that the advice it contained was not taken seriously and it was consigned to the bin. The Earth itself is shown as a dried-out, dead planet with cracked sea-beds where the oceans used to be. Only a small pool of water remains where the Atlantic Ocean once was.

The aliens looking at the dead Earth are commenting on mankind's stupidity in refusing to acknowledge and deal with the threats posed to the planet's survival. By ignoring the warning signs – represented here by the Stern Report – and by refusing to act to stop climate change, mankind proved itself not to be 'intelligent enough' to survive.

. . . . . .

Sample Answer B

The type of newspaper is not stated here, so you could decide to write for a broadsheet or a tabloid. The important thing to remember is to stick to one style and to refer to the issues raised in the cartoon.

Read the question carefully. The article is to appear on the front page of *The Martian Times*, so you would expect it to be a news article rather than a feature article.

The Martian Times
Saturday, 9 April 2214

What On Earth ...?
A lovely planet has become a lonely planet as Earth finally succumbs to the enemy within
by Zarg Xnzh

When visual elements of the cartoon are described, their meaning is explained

Verbal element is examined

Even when discussing a cartoon, you can use quotes to support your answer

Give the name of the paper, a headline and a byline

You can write a subheading if you wish

This is written as a news article, so the main point is made in the first paragraph

Life on Earth is no more. Humankind's greed and short-sightedness has finally and fatally wounded their beautiful, bountiful home. The last creature on that blighted planet has died. Now all that is left is parched earth and cracked, dry sea-beds.

Each subsequent paragraph elaborates on the topic a little more

Reporters from around the universe converged on this solar system last night, watching and mourning as the last life-form gave up its struggle to survive in the Earth's polluted, baking atmosphere. From the Earth's outer orbit, the view that was once breathtaking is now heartbreaking. No more green forests, no more lush jungles, no more sparkling oceans. No more life.

Had this annihilation been the work of an enemy planet, it might have been more understandable, if equally sad. But the realisation that it was the planet's own inhabitants who brought about this wanton destruction is something that is hard to take in. 'An A-class planet, supporting intelligent life.' That is how the Ultimate Guide to the Universe described Earth, only a few dozen years ago. Next year's entry will read somewhat differently: 'A dead planet, killed by the neglect and greed of its supposedly intelligent inhabitants.'

It is important to refer to some of the elements of the cartoon in your answer

As we turned our space ship for home last night, a copy of the Stern Report fluttered briefly in our wake. Sir Nicholas Stern was not stern enough, it seems. Let us live and learn from the example of our arrogant neighbours. If they had learned, maybe they would have lived.

SECTION 4, **PAPER 1, JUNIOR CERT HL, 2009**

1. Look at the advertisement for RTÉ 2fm opposite.

(a) Based on your reading of the advertisement, identify the target audience it is aimed at and explain how you arrived at this conclusion. You must refer to the advertisement in your answer. (20 marks)

(b) There is a perception that many young people only want to

listen to music-based radio. Based on your experience of Media Studies, what do you think would make talk-radio more attractive to young people? (20 marks)

Sample Answer 1

1(a). Based on your reading of the advertisement, identify the target audience it is aimed at and explain how you arrived at this conclusion. You must refer to the advertisement in your answer. (20)

State your point of view clearly and concisely

I think that the target audience for this advertisement is people in their teens or early twenties.

As this is a twenty-mark question, you should try to make four points if possible

The first indication that the advertisement is aimed at younger people is the type of shoe that is shown in the picture. Converse runners, particularly in this bright shade of green, are popular with young adults. The shoes are in poor condition, scuffed and worn on the heel and the sole. They look as if they have been well-used and perhaps the idea is that they have been worn to concerts or festivals.

Deal with each aspect of the advertisement separately. Try not to repeat yourself

This idea is picked up again in the slogan on the sole of the upturned shoe. It says: 'The Best Live Music Only On RTÉ 2fm'. The majority of those who attend live music events while wearing casual shoes like these are young adults.

Use advertising terminology such as 'logo' and 'slogan'

The logo in the top left-hand corner adds to the impression that the advertisement is aimed at a relatively young audience. The combination of wellies and music suggests open-air concerts and festivals. The slogan which accompanies this logo: 'Livin' the life, Lovin' the music' is written in informal language. The final letters of the words 'living' and 'loving' have been dropped, which reflects the speech patterns often associated with teenagers and young adults.

Brief summary and conclusion

This is a casual, relaxed advertisement for a music-based radio station. Such stations are generally popular with younger audiences. The combination of the verbal and visual elements in this advertisement leads me to believe that it is aimed at such a group.

Sample Answer 2

1(b). There is a perception that many young people only want to listen to music-based radio. Based on your experience of Media Studies, what do you think would make talk-radio more attractive to young people? (20)

In order for talk-based radio to become more attractive to young people the programmes would need to deal with issues of interest to a more youthful audience. If programmes covered topics such as education from the students' point of view (perhaps giving exam advice and tips), discussions of books and films popular with teenagers, reports of inter-schools sporting events and information about upcoming events which might be popular with young people, they might listen to more talk-radio.

The presenters of many talk-radio programmes are middle-aged or older. Presenters in their early twenties would be more appealing and have more credibility with a younger audience. Two or more presenters could work together, giving a more conversational atmosphere and creating some relaxed chat and banter.

Young people are used to interacting with the media nowadays. The internet is a huge draw because teenagers can chat to one another via social networking sites and are not required to sit passively and watch or listen to others holding forth. Radio programmes could capitalise on this by encouraging lots of audience participation. Listeners could phone or text or send messages via the station's Facebook page and their views could be shared live with other young people.

Regular competitions are a great way to attract a young audience to talk-radio. The best way to ensure that an audience stays tuned in is to vary the times of the competitions or to occasionally give clues to the correct answer during the course of the programme. The prizes should be relevant to young people: concert tickets or vouchers for fashionable shops, for example.

Explain why you think each suggestion would be appealing to young people

Your suggestions should be reasonable, realistic, and should show an understanding of the target audience

I believe that young people would be more than willing to listen to talk-radio should the changes I have outlined be implemented.

OR

2. Look at the information about the on-screen classification of television programmes provided on the page opposite.

(a) Explain fully the term watershed as it applies to the on-screen classification system. (10 marks)

(b) Explain what kinds of programmes can be shown before the watershed. (10 marks)

(c) Give reasons why you do or do not think that the classification system is a good idea. (20 marks)

Sample Answer 1

2(a). Explain fully the term watershed as it applies to the on-screen classification system. (10)

You must define the term 'watershed' but you must also explain it in the context of the information given in the source paper

This is a ten-mark question, so it would be appropriate to make two points

The word 'watershed' means a point which marks a division. In terms of the on-screen classification system, this means that before this time, 9pm, the programmes shown are suitable for a general audience or for young people supervised by adults. After this time, the programmes shown may be suitable only for a more mature audience who would require no adult supervision.

The idea of the watershed is to allow viewers to have control over their choice of scheduled programmes. Knowing that this point in time marks the beginning of programmes about which parents or guardians may need to make 'informed decisions whether to view or not to view' gives viewers greater control.

RTÉ On-Screen Programme Classification System

From November 2001, viewers of RTÉ One and Network 2 will have noticed small icons in the top left hand corner of their screens. The icons appear for 20 seconds at the start of programmes. This signals the beginning of a unique initiative which will see RTÉ gradually move to a situation where most programmes will be classified as to content.

The system is an information service to television viewers, letting them know more about the content of scheduled programmes so that they can make informed decisions whether to view or not to view. Children's and young adults' programmes will be labelled as such. Programmes more suited to a mature audience will not merely be scheduled after the 9.00 pm watershed, but will also be flagged on-screen.

There will be five classes:

 General Audience (GA)
a programme that would be acceptable to all ages and tastes.

 Children (Ch)
a programme aimed specifically at children,
pre-teenage or a very young teenage audience.

 Young Adult (YA)
a programme aimed at a teenage audience.

 Parental Supervision (PS)
a programme aimed at a mature audience.

 Mature Audience (MA)
a typical 'post-watershed' programme.

Sample Answer 2

2(b). Explain what kinds of programmes can be shown before the watershed. (10)

You are asked to 'explain' what kinds of programme may be shown before the watershed, so you should go into a certain amount of detail. However, this is a ten-mark question, so it should not take you longer than eight to ten minutes to answer

Before the watershed, programmes suitable for a general audience (GA) or for younger people in the company of responsible adults (PS) may be shown. Such programmes would not be expected to contain graphic or explicit violence, sexuality, bad language or any other content which may only be suitable for a mature audience. Pre-watershed programmes might include anything from children's shows such as Barney *and* Dora the Explorer *to soap operas containing a moderate amount of mature content.*

Certain scheduled programmes may be aimed at a mature audience but may be viewed by children who are in the company of their parents. These programmes will be flagged as 'PS', meaning 'Parental Supervision', and may be shown before the watershed.

. . . . . .

Sample Answer 3

2(c). Give reasons why you do or do not think that the classification system is a good idea. (20)

You are free to agree or disagree with the classification system. Below are two sample answers, one in favour of the system and one disagreeing with it. Remember, you are not being judged on your opinion, but rather on your ability to express that opinion. If you argue your case well, you will get a high mark. There are no rights and wrongs here.

I think the classification system is a good idea because it allows parents and guardians to decide which programmes are suitable for younger viewers, it is straightforward and easy to understand, it allows viewers and their parents greater freedom, and it can guard against children encountering films or programmes which might cause them distress.

Realistically, parents and guardians do not have time to sit in the room with children, ensuring that every programme is suitable for young people. Thanks to this classification system, all they now need to do is stay in the room for the first twenty seconds of the programme and look at the icon which appears in the top left-hand corner. Once they know that the programme is 'GA', meaning 'acceptable to all ages and tastes', for example, they can leave the room with a clear conscience.

The fact that there are only five categories of programme is a good thing. This makes the system very user-friendly. Parents and guardians may not always know whether or not a particular series or film is appropriate for a particular age group, but a quick glance at the icon should inform them as to the content of the piece.

The classification system should also ensure that parents and children can have greater control over viewing matter. Children and teenagers can now assure those in charge that the programmes they want to watch are age-appropriate. This means that young people can watch such programmes in relative peace.

Finally, I feel that such a classification system will prevent many children from being exposed to material which could cause them distress. Once parents are alerted to the fact that a certain programme may contain material aimed at a more mature audience, they can decide to stop very young children from viewing it, or decide to sit in the room and supervise older children's viewing.

. . . . . .

Alternative Sample Answer 3

I do not think the classification system is a good idea because it reduces parental responsibility, it assumes that those who make

Main points are outlined in the opening paragraph. This paragraph is optional: the answer would be complete without it but it can make the examiner's life easier

Each point is more fully developed

Each point is dealt with in turn, in the same order in which they were outlined in the opening paragraph

the classification judgements are correct, and the appearance of the icons on the screen is of too short a duration to have any real effect.

Parents and guardians should be the people to decide what children should watch. They know whether or not their children are mature enough to be positively or negatively affected by what is shown on television. Sometimes a programme might be flagged as inappropriate because it contains scenes of violence, but if this is in the context of a documentary on some important period in history, parents might feel that the violence is justified and that the children could learn from watching it.

Classification is a reflection of the moral and political views of those in authority. It is a short step from classification to censorship and propaganda. There are books and films on the English syllabus nowadays which might well have been censored in our grandparents' lifetimes. Of Mice And Men and To Kill A Mockingbird are popular texts for Junior Certificate study, but the book and film versions of both were and are banned in many school districts in America to this day.

Finally, I feel that flashing an icon in the top corner of the screen for twenty seconds is ineffective. It relies on parents or guardians being in the room for those vital moments. This is unrealistic. The idea of classification may be well-intentioned, but the reality is at best pointless and at worst oppressive.

Although it is best to think in terms of '5 marks = 1 well-developed point', you should not repeat yourself or make invalid points just to reach this quota. The examiner will be well qualified to make a judgement on your answer, and three strong points are better than four weak ones

UNSEEN DRAMA

*The Unseen Drama section of Paper 2 is worth **30 marks**.*

*You should spend about **25 minutes** on this section.*

The usual format is three 15-mark questions, of which you must choose two. However, this can change, so make sure you read the questions carefully and take note of the marks awarded to each one.

MARKING ✓

Total: **30**

In the Unseen Drama section you have to answer questions on an extract from a play that you have not studied. One of the extracts will be from a Shakespearean drama and the other from a more modern play. Many people are put off by Shakespearean plays, but it is worth considering this option, particularly if you have studied a Shakespearean play for the Junior Cert. Don't worry if you don't understand every single word; there will be a glossary at the end of the extract giving the meanings of any words that are vital to the understanding of the piece.

EXAM **FOCUS** *When you read the introduction to the extract, try to visualise each of the characters and their positions on stage. As you read through the extract, try to imagine each character saying the lines aloud.*

Shakespearean drama can be divided into three main categories: comedies, tragedies and historical dramas. In general, the extract given will focus on a key moment in the play, often highlighting conflict between two characters. If you have studied Shakespeare already, you will know that the themes he deals with are love, jealousy, revenge, war and so forth; in other words, fairly universal themes that should be easy to understand.

The Shakespearean extract is usually a reasonably easy one and the questions are fairly straightforward, so if you have studied his work in school, it would be well worth considering this option.

You don't really have time to read both extracts carefully and then make a choice, so think about it and decide which one you will attempt between now and the exam.

It is advisable to read all the questions following both extracts before making a decision.

It is very unlikely that the extract selected for the unseen question will be from a play you have studied for your Junior Cert. If this is the case, however, you should avoid this unseen option and choose the more modern play instead. It can happen that students know the unseen plays (perhaps through drama classes, for example) and in that case, they should be very careful to base their answer only on the extract given.

'All the world's a stage …'

If you are studying Shakespeare in school and find the language difficult, answer the 'Other Drama' question.

EXAM **FOCUS**

The 'Other Drama' option offers you the opportunity to answer questions based on a more modern play. The questions are generally similar to those on Shakespearean drama; and, as with the Shakespeare questions, if you know the play, be sure to base your answer only on the extract.

TYPICAL QUESTIONS AND HOW TO APPROACH THEM

Character

There is usually a question which asks what you have learned about the character. Play the role of detective when you are looking for hints. Look at what the characters say and do and what other people tell us about them. Read the introduction to the extract very carefully. It gives you valuable information which you can use in your answer and sets you on the right path in terms of character analysis. Look at the following example from the 2007 Paper.

Background to this extract

Katharina is the wild, rough and troublesome elder daughter of Baptista. Baptista wants to find a husband for her. He has arranged a marriage with Petruchio, a nobleman. In this extract Katharina and Petruchio have just met for the first time.

Note: In Shakespeare's time a woman with a scolding or nagging nature was called a **shrew**.

EXAM **FOCUS**   *The word 'impression' usually means that the question is about character.*

SECTION 1 (A), **PAPER 2, JUNIOR CERT HL, 2007**

1. What is your impression of Katharina from this extract? Support your answer with reference to the text. (15 marks)

Even before we read the extract itself, we are given valuable information which will help in answering Question 1. Obviously, it is important to use your own words; it would not be a good idea to simply repeat the description given in the introduction. You would also need to go through the text, finding evidence for this description of Katharina, but the introduction is certainly a help and sets you on the right path.

Relationships

You may be asked about the relationship between the characters in the extract you are given. Again, look at the introduction for clues as well as studying what the characters say to and about each other. Stage directions can help here: if someone moves away from someone else, what might it suggest?

Note

The questions on character and relationships may be framed in terms of a personal response: you may be asked which of the characters you would like to have as a friend, and why. Or you may be asked how you think the character would feel about the actions in the extract and the behaviour of those around them. Such questions may seem vague, but you are expected to base your answer on what you have read and to support your points with quotation and/or reference.

Ask yourself what type of question each one is, for example: 'This question asks me if I would like to be stranded on a desert island with Person X, so it's a question about character.'   EXAM **FOCUS**

Staging the scene

This is a very common question in the unseen drama section of the paper. You may be asked how you would stage this scene, possibly even in a time or place different from that in the original extract. Refer to the text to support the staging choices you make. Think about each of the following:

Set

It is not necessary to describe an elaborate set. A few pieces of furniture and a simple backdrop can do the job perfectly adequately. For example, if the scene takes place in a family kitchen, a table, several chairs, perhaps a dresser, a cooker or a fire (depending on the era) would be enough.

EXAM **FOCUS**   *Remember that when it comes to staging, less is more. Sets and props should be able to be removed/assembled quickly. Don't give details of tiny props as the audience will be unlikely to see them.*

Stage positioning

Would you place a character in a position of dominance and power – perhaps in a higher position than the other characters if you had a tiered stage – or would you have him or her standing alone and isolated from the rest of the cast?

Posture

Would you have the characters standing proudly upright or bent in humble submission? Would they make exaggerated gestures and speak loudly or would they whisper and creep around the stage? Whatever posture you choose tells the examiner what you think about the character. Refer to the extract to support your choices.

EXAM **FOCUS**   *Body language is related to character. Look closely at the extract for clues as to how the character might behave.*

Facial expression

This can tell us a lot about the characters' true feelings. They might show exasperation by sighing, raising their eyebrows and shaking their heads, or they might smile cruelly at the discomfort of others, for example.

Costumes and make-up

Again, how you choose to use these gives a good indication of what you think of the characters and what is happening to them in the play. Torn, dishevelled clothes and a dirty face tell a very different story from fine silks and jewels and beautifully coiffured hair. Colours can also be very suggestive: red can mean passion or anger; white can signal purity or innocence; and black is commonly used to show that a character is evil. Pale make-up may suggest ill health or shock, while yellow or greenish tinges to the skin tone can be indicative of sinister, evil qualities. These are only suggestions; obviously you are free to choose from a wide variety of options when it comes to costumes and make-up. It is the one instance where you are hoping that people will judge a book by its cover. Use plenty of adjectives here: torn, dishevelled, sleek, expensive, flowing, tightly fitted, bloody, etc.

EXAM **FOCUS**

Refer back to the Media Studies chapter to see what colours are associated with different moods, character traits or atmospheres.

Sound effects

Music is the most obvious tool here; it can be romantic, sorrowful or uplifting, echoing the mood of the scene. Your choice will tell the examiner whether or not you have understood the mood. In Shakespearean drama, the arrival of the king or other important personages is often heralded by the sound of trumpets. As actors in Shakespeare's time were very limited in terms of set and props, much of the action in his plays happens off-stage. Characters often appear on-stage with tales of battles being fought, which could be backed up by the sound of swords clashing and ringing, and the shouts and screams of the fighting and injured men.

Lighting

Good lighting can also be most effective in establishing mood or atmosphere. Think about the possible use of spotlights to pick out the important characters, filters to create warm, glowing light or dim light to create a menacing or eerie atmosphere.

Continue the story ...

You may be asked to continue the story in your own words. If the extract is Shakespearean, you will not be required to use iambic pentameter or Early Modern English, but you should stick to the atmosphere of the piece and have the characters behave in a way that is consistent with what you have read in the extract. This is a difficult option for many students and best avoided if you have not practised this in advance and had guidance and correction from your teacher.

Mood or atmosphere

You may be asked if you think the extract is happy, sad, tense, light-hearted or serious. Look through the extract for clues and remember that if the question asks whether the extract is 'happy or sad or a mixture of both', there will be evidence of both happiness and sadness in the piece. You would be well-advised to choose the 'mixture of both' option here as it would give you more to write about.

- Look out for stage directions which may tell you something about the characters' moods.
- If the actor is instructed to speak in a raised voice or to slam a cup down on the table, this is an obvious sign that he or she is angry or frustrated.
- When it comes to the dialogue, watch out for misunderstandings between characters. This can indicate tension but it can also be comic.
- Short, clipped answers to questions can indicate that a character does not want to discuss a topic. This can show that the mood is tense.
- Look at the dynamic between the various characters. Is it a case of two ganging up on a third? Is one person bullying another? Is one character trying to make the peace?

As a general rule, the easiest questions are those which can be answered by direct reference to the extract. The less you have to invent, the better.

SECTION 1 (A), **PAPER 2, JUNIOR CERT HL, 2007**

The following extract (in edited form) is taken from The Taming of the Shrew *by William Shakespeare. Read the extract carefully and then answer the questions which follow.*

Background to this extract

Katharina is the wild, rough and troublesome elder daughter of Baptista. Baptista wants to find a husband for her. He has arranged a marriage with Petruchio, a nobleman. In this extract Katharina and Petruchio have just met for the first time.

Note: In Shakespeare's time a woman with a scolding or nagging nature was called a **shrew**.

PETRUCHIO: *[He seizes her in his arms]* Nay, come, Kate, come; you must not look so sour.

KATHARINA: *[She struggles]* It is my fashion when I see a crab.*

PETRUCHIO: Why, here's no crab, and therefore look not sour.

KATHARINA: There is, there is.

PETRUCHIO: Then show it me.

KATHARINA: Had I a glass I would.

PETRUCHIO: What, you mean my face? By Saint George, I am too young for you.

KATHARINA: Yet you are withered.

PETRUCHIO: *[Kisses her hand]* 'Tis with cares.

KATHARINA: *[She slips from him]* I care not!

PETRUCHIO: Nay, hear you Kate. In sooth, you escape not so.
[He catches her once more]

KATHARINA: I'll scrape you if I tarry. Let me go!
*[She struggles again, biting and scratching
as he speaks]*

PETRUCHIO: No, not a whit – I find you passing gentle:
'Twas told me you were rough and coy and sullen,
And now I find reports of you untrue;
For thou art pleasant, lively, passing courteous,
But slow in speech; yet sweet as spring-time flowers.
Thou canst not frown, thou canst not look unkindly,
Nor bite the lip, as angry wenches will,
Nor hast thou pleasure to be cross in talk;
But thou with mildness entertain'st thy admirers,
With gentle ways, soft and agreeable. *[He releases her]*
Kate like the hazel-twig
Is straight and slender, and as brown in hue
As hazel-nuts and sweeter than the kernels …

KATHARINA: Go, fool! Order your servants about, not me.

PETRUCHIO: Did ever the Goddess Diana so grace a place
As Kate this chamber with her noble ways?
O, be thou Diana and let her be Kate.

KATHARINA: Where did you study all this goodly speech?

PETRUCHIO: It comes naturally, from my mother-wit.

KATHARINA: A witty mother! And without wit her son!

PETRUCHIO: Setting all this chat aside, your father hath consented
That you shall be my wife; your dowry agreed on;
And you, willing or not, will marry me.
Now, Kate, I am a husband fit for you

For by this light whereby I see thy beauty,
  – Thy beauty that doth make me like thee well –
Thou must be married to no man but me.
For I am born to tame you, Kate,
And bring you from a wild Kate to a Kate
As kind as other household Kates.

crab: crab-apple, sour fruit

*Answer **two** of the following questions. Each question is worth **15 marks**.*

1. What is your impression of Katharina from this extract? Support your answer with reference to the text.

2. Do you think Petruchio's way of speaking to Katharina would encourage her to marry him? Base your answer on this extract.

3. Imagine that you are directing this play. In the context of the extract you have read above give your thoughts on two of the following aspects of your production: use of voice, costuming, setting, movement on stage.

Sample Answer 1

1. What is your impression of Katharina from this extract? Support your answer with reference to the text. (15)

This is a question about character. If you are asked to give your impression of someone, you must use words which describe their character. Don't simply say what they do or say, but explain what this tells us about them. As this is a 15-mark question, you should aim to make three well-developed points about Katharina. Each point should have a separate paragraph. You could choose to develop one aspect of Katharina's character, but that is a tall order and can be difficult to sustain over a page or so of your answer book. A few points, well supported, is an easier option.

Remember the key ways to find out about a person's character in a drama extract:

1. What they say
2. What they do
3. What others say about them
4. How others act in their presence

These are the main points about Katharina's character which will be addressed in the answer. Several of them will be dealt with together as they are closely linked

Try to work the quotes into the body of the answer rather than letting them stand alone

My impression of Katharina is that she is unkind, insulting, strong-willed, difficult, wild, rough and troublesome.

Katharina's unkind and insulting nature is seen early in the *extract. She compares Petruchio to a crab-apple, which is hardly a kind thing to say. When he defends himself and claims that he is* 'too young for you', *she continues to insult him, saying, 'Yet you are withered.' Later on in the extract she calls Petruchio a fool and someone who is 'without wit'. Her treatment of Petruchio seems cruel, particularly as he is only complimenting her.*

Katharina's strong will comes to the fore when she refuses to accept any of Petruchio's compliments. He makes a long speech in which he flatters her outrageously, calling her 'pleasant, lively, passing courteous' and 'soft and agreeable', among other things. She is unmoved by all of this sweet talk and says harshly, 'Go, fool! Order your servants about, not me.' It is clear that Katharina's mind is her own. She cannot be easily swayed and she asks Petruchio where he has learned 'all this goodly speech'. She is not impressed by fine words and says that she sees through Petruchio's smooth talk.

We should not be surprised that Katharina appears so difficult as the introduction to the extract tells us that she is the 'wild, rough and troublesome' daughter of Baptista. Petruchio seems to have heard this description of her too, as he says, ''Twas told me you were rough and coy and sullen.' Katharina's rude response to Petruchio's flattery and her threat of physical violence, should her

[handwritten: insults him further]

suitor keep hold of her, *'I'll scrape you if I tarry,'* tells us that she is not a gentle, peaceable person. The stage directions at this point in the extract inform us that Katharina is *'biting and scratching'* her prospective husband. This adds weight to the impression of her as a rough and difficult woman.

I think that Petruchio has his work cut out for him in the taming of this aptly named *'shrew'*.

If you get a chance to mention the stage directions, do so. It shows you understand that this is a piece of drama

Personal opinion is woven into the brief conclusion

Sample Answer 2

2. Do you think Petruchio's way of speaking to Katharina would encourage her to marry him? Base your answer on this extract. (15)

You are free to agree or disagree with this statement, as long as you can support your answer with quotation from or reference to the extract.

Yes, I think that Petruchio's way of speaking would encourage Katharina to marry him because he is flattering, romantic and persistent.

Petruchio appears captivated by Katharina and he seems to disagree with others' assessment of her. He says that, despite having heard bad reports of her from others, he finds her 'pleasant, lively, passing courteous'. Even if Katharina knows that he is flattering her for his own purposes, his words are romantic and persuasive.

This romantic vision of Katharina is emphasised further when Petruchio compares her to 'the Goddess Diana' and says that her very presence graces the room. He is wonderfully descriptive when he lists her attributes. To him, she is 'straight and slender' as the hazel twig, and 'sweeter than the kernels' of that tree. It seems that he can see nothing but goodness in the object of his affection. It would take a very romantic man to overcome the objections of a woman as strong-minded as Katharina, and I believe Petruchio is that man. He persists in his declarations of love, despite her

The main points are outlined in the opening sentence

The paragraphs are linked to one another whenever possible

repeated declarations of dislike. He says that he is 'a husband fit for you', and insists that she must be married to no other man. I feel that this determination in the face of such open hostility is bound to pay off eventually.

Sample Answer 3

3. Imagine that you are directing this play. In the context of the extract you have read above give your thoughts on two of the following aspects of your production: use of voice, costuming, setting, movement on stage. (15)

You can choose any two aspects of production, but you must justify your choices. Remember, this is a question on drama and you will have to support everything you say with quotation from or reference to the extract.

Explain your choice. You could use modern or period costume: either would be fine

The two aspects of production on which I am going to focus are costuming and use of voice.

I would dress both Katharina and Petruchio in modern costumes as I feel that an audience would relate to such clothing.

Katharina's clothes should reflect both her status and her rebellious attitude. I would dress her in designer jeans and a bright red pullover. Red signals danger and passion, both of which are appropriate for a woman who says to Petruchio, 'I'll scrape you if I tarry.' The cut of the jeans and top would be quite masculine as Katharina does not appear to be a woman who wishes to emphasise her femininity and she is unmoved by Petruchio's praise of her beauty.

Details such as colour are important

Petruchio's costume should be expensive and well-cut, as he is a nobleman. I would dress him in a black suit with a white shirt and a red tie. Black is a colour which can signify power and wealth, which would be appropriate for Petruchio. The red tie would complement Katharina's red top and this would link the characters visually.

In this instance, it is better to give each character a separate paragraph as they are being discussed separately

I would tell Petruchio to speak in a smooth, relaxed, good-

natured way when flattering Katharina. He should sound romantic and persuasive when he asks rhetorically, 'Did ever the Goddess Diana so grace a place/As Kate this chamber with her noble ways?' However, when Katharina continues to resist his advances, he should speak in a firmer, more serious tone of voice and say definitely, 'Thou must be married to no man but me. / For I am born to tame you, Kate.'

Katharina should vary between sounding angry and contemptuous. When she pours scorn on Petruchio's 'goodly speech' and advises him not to order her about, Katharina should speak in a loud, mocking voice. Her tone should be imperative when she tells Petruchio to leave her alone, telling him 'I'll scratch thee if I tarry'. As she is 'wild, rough and troublesome', Katharina's voice should rise to a shout when she feels she is being ignored. Both she and Petruchio are strong, powerful characters in their own right and their voices and costumes should reflect this.

Make sure to use plenty of descriptive words for both costume and voice

SECTION 1 (B), PAPER 2, JUNIOR CERT HL, 2010

The following extract (in edited form) is adapted from a play Same Old Moon *by Geraldine Aron. Read the extract carefully and answer the questions which follow*

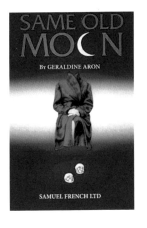

Background to this extract

In this extract we meet Brenda Barnes, just home from Australia. She is visiting her widowed mother Bridie and her Aunt Peace, who live together.

Also on stage we see the ghost of Desmond, Bridie's late husband and Brenda's father. Although he reacts to the women's conversation, Desmond says nothing during this extract.

1980s. The stage is split in two – a small cramped living room and a bedroom section which is occupied by Desmond's ghost. The ghost reacts from time to time but is generally still and inconspicuous. Bridie has prepared a tea-trolley; she enters with the milk jug, and puts it on the trolley

BRENDA: New curtains, Mum? They're lovely.

BRIDIE: Thanks, love.

PEACE: I was just thinking to myself that if you weren't going to notice them we'd wasted our time making them. I thought you'd say something the minute you came in.

BRENDA: *(Reasonably)* Give us a chance. I mean they don't exactly jump out at a person. They're exactly the same as the old ones … *(Uncertainly)* aren't they?

BRIDIE: These are mushroom. The old ones were beige. We might as well have kept them if you can't see the difference. Well, I must say Brenda, I thought you were more observant. Not a word about the new tea-trolley.

(Bridie hands out cups of tea, first to Peace, then to Brenda)

BRIDIE: Here we are now. Sugar's in.

BRENDA: Sorry to be such a pest, Mum, but I don't take milk or sugar in mine.

BRIDIE: Oh? Since when?

BRENDA: About fifteen years.

BRIDIE: Well, that's strange. Because it's the first I've heard of it.

PEACE: Throw it down the drain if she doesn't want it.

BRIDIE: Black tea. Out of the blue. You remind me of your father, pretending to like his meat underdone.

(The light comes up on Desmond 'the ghost'. He becomes alert and reacts now that he is being discussed)

BRENDA: (Smiling) Maybe he really did like his meat underdone.

(Desmond reacts)

BRIDIE: Indeed he did not. That was all put on, trying to impress people.

(Desmond reacts)

PEACE: It's probably smart, in Australia, but can you imagine what black tea does to the lining of your stomach?

BRIDIE: The tannin you mean? Sure tannin is more poisonous than nicotine.

BRENDA: (Showing strain) I'll drink it, OK? No problem at all. (She drains her cup and slams cup and saucer down on the trolley)

BRIDIE: (Wounded) There was no need for that, Brenda. No need at all. How were we supposed to know you suddenly stopped taking milk and sugar? We'll know for the next time.

BRENDA: That's OK then.

PEACE: Bridie and I had a great idea, to simplify our tea drinking. I used to take two sugars and Bridie used to take one. So we split the difference and now we both take one and half and it doesn't matter if the cups get mixed up. Aren't we sensible?

BRENDA: (Smiling) Very sensible.

Answer **two** of the following questions. Each question is worth **15 marks**.

1. From your reading of the extract, what kind of relationship exists between Brenda and her mother, Bridie? Support your

answer with reference to the extract.

2. In your opinion is this extract serious or humorous or a mixture of both? Explain your answer with reference to the extract.

3. The ghost, Desmond, reacts three times in the course of this extract. In each of these three cases explain why he reacts.

What effect do you think his reactions would have on an audience?

Sample Answer 1

1. From your reading of the extract, what kind of relationship exists between Brenda and her mother, Bridie? Support your answer with reference to the extract. (15)

The type of relationship is clearly defined at the outset

From my reading of the extract, I think the relationship between Brenda and her mother, Bridie, is a difficult one.

On the surface, it would appear that Brenda and Bridie want

As this question is worth 15 marks, you should aim to make three well-developed points

to get on. Brenda makes the effort to visit her mother and her mother offers her tea. Brenda opens the conversation on a positive note, admiring the new curtains. Almost immediately, however, things deteriorate as Bridie appears injured by the fact that Brenda did not admire the curtains as soon as she entered the room. Bridie twists the conversation around so that Brenda's delay in commenting on the curtains, and her failure to spot the new tea-trolley, quickly becomes a way for her mother to make a little attack on Brenda's personality: 'Well, I must say Brenda, I thought you were more observant.'

Note the way in which each point is supported with reference to and quotation from the passage

The tension increases as the conversation continues. Brenda's preference for black tea is scorned by her mother, who clearly considers it an affectation. She compares it to her late husband's liking for underdone meat, which she says was 'all put on'. The stage directions here add to our impression that the relationship between mother and daughter is a strained, unhappy one. Brenda drinks her tea quickly and 'slams cup and saucer down on the trolley'. Bridie is described as 'wounded' by this behaviour.

It is obvious that Bridie and Brenda are not close and do not know each other very well. Brenda has been drinking her tea black for fifteen years, but Bridie says, 'It's the first I've heard of it.' Perhaps this is understandable, considering Brenda lives in Australia, but it adds to our impression that their relationship is not an intimate or a happy one.

The conclusion refers back to the question

Sample Answer 2

2. In your opinion is this extract serious or humorous or a mixture of both? Explain your answer with reference to the extract.(15)

If you are ever presented with a question which invites you to discuss both options in the same answer, you should do so. For example, this question clearly paves the way for you to discuss both the serious and the humorous aspects of the given extract.

I think this extract presents a serious topic in a humorous way. Bridie's comment about the colour of the curtains, when she chides Brenda for not noticing them sooner, is an amusing one. As readers, we sympathise with Brenda and are entertained by the notion that there could be a visible difference between the two colours Bridie mentions: mushroom and beige. The fact that she follows up this remark by accusing Brenda of not saying 'a word about the new tea-trolley' adds to the humour here. Obviously Bridie replaces old things with almost identical new ones and is surprised and hurt when nobody spots the difference.

The opening paragraph states that both the serious and the humorous aspects of the extract will be dealt with in this extract

The other characters in the extract add to the humorous tone. Desmond, the ghost, reacts to Bridie's remark that he only pretended to like his meat underdone because, she claims, he was 'trying to impress people'. That anybody should do such a thing or the idea that anyone would actually be impressed by someone eating underdone meat is clearly ludicrous, and Desmond's

These paragraphs deal with the humorous aspect of the extract

reaction brings that to our attention. He adds to the sense of the ridiculous in the piece. Aunt Peace does the same. She and Bridie are like a double act, conspiring against poor Brenda. Their belief that black tea may be considered 'smart' in Australia but is actually 'more poisonous than nicotine' is very amusing, as is their decision to reach a compromise on the amount of sugar they have in their tea.

This paragraph addresses the more serious aspects of the extract

Although the dialogue is entertaining, the underlying message is a serious one. Here we see a mother and a daughter who have a very poor relationship, and we sense that the ghost, Desmond, was unhappy and misunderstood when he was alive. Aunt Peace belies her name, and adds to the sense of tension. She criticises Brenda whenever she gets the chance and supports Bridie in her nonsensical ideas.

The conclusion pulls both sides of the argument together

The conversation we are presented with in this extract may be funny, but we are left with a sense of sadness at the lack of real communication between the various family members.

Sample Answer 3

3. The ghost, Desmond, reacts three times in the course of this extract. In each of these three cases explain why he reacts.

What effect do you think his reactions would have on an audience? (15)

Read this question carefully. There are two parts to it. You must explain why Desmond reacts in each case **and** comment on the effect this would have on the audience.

Words and phrases such as 'amused' and 'taken aback' show the effect of the reactions on the audience

Desmond, the ghost, first reacts when he hears his name mentioned by Bridie. He is stirred by hearing her discussing the fact that he liked his meat underdone and speaking quite scornfully of him. I think the audience might be a little taken aback initially to see the ghost move, but they would soon realise that his reaction is merely a denial of Bridie's nonsensical claim that he only pretended to like his meat that way. When the audience realised this, they would be amused.

The second time Desmond reacts is when he hears Brenda defending his preference for underdone meat. Clearly, he agrees with her and is pleased that someone understands him. The effect of this on the audience would be twofold, I think. They would be saddened for Desmond when they realised how misunderstood he was by his own wife, and their belief that Bridie was being ridiculous would be strengthened by the ghost's reaction.

Desmond's final reaction in this extract is to Bridie's remark about his 'trying to impress people' by liking underdone meat. Again, I feel that his reaction would highlight for the audience how ludicrous Bridie's claim is, and it would probably make them laugh aloud.

Try to vary your vocabulary as much as possible

Overall, I think Desmond's reactions would reinforce the mood of the extract, which is a mixture of humour and sadness. He would seem to be supporting Brenda's view of her mother as unreasonable and more than a little foolish. The audience might be a little startled when he first reacts, but they would soon see the meaning behind his sudden movement.

balance the mood of

STUDIED DRAMA

The Studied Drama section of Paper 2 is worth **30 marks**.

You should spend about **25 minutes** on this section.

EXAM **FOCUS** *Plays are meant to be seen, not read. Obviously, you have to read them for the Junior Cert exam, but you should also make a real effort to see a stage production or, at the very least, you should watch a DVD of the play.*

TYPICAL QUESTIONS AND HOW TO PREPARE FOR THEM

When you are studying your chosen play, you should ensure that you are able to discuss each of the following:

Character

You should have reasonably detailed notes on each of the main characters. Try to organise these notes under headings so that, when you come to revise them, you will be able to scan quickly through the headings and remind yourself of the main points about each character. For example, if you were preparing notes on Romeo's character, you might use the following headings:

- Moody
- Changeable
- Dramatic
- Passionate
- Reckless
- Brave
- Loyal

You might also want to consider whether your chosen characters are **dynamic** or **static**. If they are dynamic, they change and develop as the play progresses. If they are static, they remain the same throughout the play.

*You should be prepared to write about the **main** character in your chosen play. There is generally no need to concern yourself with minor characters. Ask yourself if you liked the character more at the end of the play than you did at the beginning. Why/why not?*

EXAM **FOCUS**

A good way to revise your chosen characters is to ask yourself the five questions shown below and try to write answers to each. Then, if you are asked to write an essay-style answer on the characters, you will be likely to structure that answer well. Ask yourself these questions in the exam, too.

1. How is the character **introduced** and what is our first impression of him or her?
2. Does the character have to face any **challenges** and if so, how does he or she react to them?
3. Does the character have to deal with a major **crisis** at a turning point in the play?
4. How is the crisis **resolved** and what role (if any) does the character play in the resolution?
5. What is our **final impression** of the character and is it different from our initial impression?

Relationships

You should be able to discuss the relationships between the major characters. Again, the five question rule will help you prepare for this question.

1. How is the relationship **introduced**?
2. Are there **challenges** or difficulties which threaten the relationship?
3. Is there a moment of **crisis** in the relationship?
4. How is the crisis **resolved**?
5. What state is the relationship in at the **end** of the play?

EXAM **FOCUS**   *Ask yourself if the characters in the relationship are better or worse people as a result of the relationship. This will tell you whether or not they have been improved by or benefited from the relationship.*

Theme

You should know the theme, or the main message, of your chosen play. Although there may be many themes in the play, you should concentrate on the major ones. Love and hate, for example, are central to *Romeo and Juliet*, while intolerance and the power of friendship are central to *The Merchant of Venice*.

At this stage, you will be unsurprised to hear that the five question rule also applies to questions on theme.

1. How is the theme **introduced**?
2. Is the theme **developed** as the characters face **challenges** or **difficulties**?
3. Is there a moment of **crisis** when the theme is clearly shown?
4. What does the **resolution** of the crisis tell us about the theme?
5. What have we learned about the theme by the **end of the play**, and what is the **final message**?

Key scenes

Think of the five questions just mentioned. Most key scenes can be found at one of these points in the play. Be prepared to discuss a scene from any of these key moments and be able to discuss the impact of this scene.

The plot is the series of events that ties the story together and gives it meaning.

Most plots can be divided into the stages seen below:

1. Exposition, or introduction to the characters and potential complications in the plot.
2. Complications, challenges and conflict.
3. Climax. The moment of greatest tension; this is usually a turning point in the action.
4. Resolution (can be happy or sad).
5. Ending. We see the final effects of the events of the play.

Staging

You may be asked how you would stage your chosen play. Refer back to the section on staging in the **Unseen Drama** section of this book (page 141).

Mood or atmosphere

You may be asked to discuss a scene which is **happy, sad, tense,** light-hearted or serious.

Conflict

Be prepared to discuss conflict between characters and have in mind a number of key scenes where this conflict is clearly shown. It is a good idea to think in terms of plot structure when answering your questions as it can help you to stay focused.

If you are asked a question on the conflict between two major characters, for example, you should look at the plot structure above and trace the conflict through each of the stages of the plot.

Depending on the question, it may not be necessary to mention every aspect of the plot. Use your own judgement here.

EXAM **FOCUS** *Remember, conflict can be verbal (Antonio and Shylock in* The Merchant of Venice, *or Juliet and her parents in* Romeo and Juliet) *or physical and verbal (Tybalt and Romeo in* Romeo and Juliet).

Social setting

You may be asked to comment on the world of the play and you should be ready to say why you would or would not like to live in that world. The sort of things you should consider are:

1. The time period in which the play is set.
2. The place where the play is set.
3. The political background, if relevant. Is there a war on, for example?
4. The way women and children are treated.
5. Is there prejudice or injustice in the world of the play?
6. What are the people's religious beliefs? Do they affect their actions?
7. Who holds the most power in the world of the play?

EXAM **FOCUS** *Think about the plot of the play for a moment. Would the events happen in Ireland in the twenty-first century? Why/why not?*

Review

Be able to say why you would recommend this play to people of your own age. Consider each of the points given above. For example, you might want to talk about the theme(s), the characters, the relationships, the dramatic effect of the play and what you learned about the world of the play. That gives you five points to discuss. You could add more, of course.

In a review, you can talk about the good and the bad aspects of the play. However, in the final paragraph you should be prepared to say what you thought of the play overall and whether you would recommend it.   EXAM **FOCUS**

PLANNING YOUR ANSWER

The examiner will not know which play you have studied so it is essential to state this in your introductory paragraph. Make sure that you spell the name of the playwright and the play correctly. A misspelling at this stage of the answer will create a bad impression.

Each paragraph should answer the question asked. At the planning stage, check back with the wording of the question each time you plan a point and make sure that you are not simply writing a summary of the plot.

In your conclusion, refer back to the question again, using different words from those you used in the introduction.

Length

Your Studied Drama answer should take up roughly two pages of your answer booklet.

Quotes

You will need to use quotes to support your answer. Keep these short and relevant. A line or two is often better than a whole speech.

EXAM **FOCUS** *If you have planned answers to the questions listed in this chapter, you should be well prepared for the exam. Stay calm on the day and examine the question closely. It may look unfamiliar, but the chances are that it will be one of the questions dealt with in this section or a combination of those questions.*

QUESTION 2, SECTION 1, PAPER 2, JUNIOR CERT HL, 2004

Name a play you have studied.
Choose a scene from this play that you found either happy **or** *sad. Describe how the playwright conveys this happiness* **or** *sadness.* (30 marks)

Note that you are **not** asked what happens in this scene but **how** the playwright uses language, stage directions, characterisation, etc. to convey happiness or sadness.

The obvious scene to choose here would be the scene in which Romeo and Juliet take their own lives, but if you can do something a little out of the ordinary – provided you can support your view – there is a better chance of your getting a higher mark.

Sample Answer

Don't forget to name the play and the playwright in the opening paragraph. If you know the number of the scene, give it. If not, describe it briefly

The play I have studied is William Shakespeare's Romeo and Juliet *and the scene which I found particularly sad was Act 3 Scene 5.*

This scene is the turning point of the play and it marks the end of Romeo and Juliet's short-lived happiness as a married couple. The scene opens with the pair about to part after their first night together. Although it is only a few days since they first met, this parting is nonetheless extremely hard for them to bear. The language at the start of this scene is simple but effective. Juliet tries to pretend that it is not yet morning and that there is no need for Romeo to leave. We feel her longing and her pain when she pretends to believe that it is 'the nightingale, and not the lark' that sings outside.

Romeo shows a more mature side of himself than we have seen so far when he insists on leaving, because he knows that to stay would mean death. His language is more straightforward than it was at the start of the play when he professed his love for Rosaline, and then for Juliet, in a flowery, extravagant way. Here he is natural and restrained and all the more believable for that. He speaks plainly, saying, 'It was the lark, the herald of the morn:/No nightingale'. This simplicity makes his speeches more hauntingly sad and beautiful than any of his earlier, overblown rhetoric ever could have.

Although both Romeo's and Juliet's words are romantic and full of love, there is a hint of death and despair in them too. The constant references to death foreshadow the tragedy that is to come. Romeo insists that he must leave or 'stay and die', but when Juliet begs him to stay he claims that he will do so and will embrace his end: 'Come, death, and welcome,' if that is what his loved one wishes. At this, Juliet changes her tune and begs him to leave. Her love and her anguish are plain to see as she agonises over their situation: 'More light and light; more dark and dark our woes!'

The young lovers' conversation is suddenly interrupted by the appearance of the Nurse, who warns Juliet that 'Your lady mother is coming to your chamber.' There is a sense of dramatic irony here as the audience knows that Capulet has agreed to give his daughter in marriage to Paris and that Juliet will soon hear this. Romeo leaves but not before promising to 'omit no opportunity/ That may convey my greetings, love, to thee'. His words do not comfort Juliet, who has a premonition of disaster. The mood is darkened once more as she claims that she has 'an ill-divining

Make sure to refer to the question in every paragraph and to comment on the sadness of the scene

Short quotes which illustrate your point are essential in an answer on the Studied Drama

Remember that you must comment on how Shakespeare makes this scene so sad

Although you can, and should, mention some of the events of the scene, you must avoid writing a summary. Everything you say must be connected to the question

soul' and can see Romeo 'As one dead in the bottom of a tomb'. Tragically, this is exactly how she will next see her husband.

Even though the audience has no way of knowing that it is the last time Romeo and Juliet will ever speak to one another, there are enough hints of the tragedy to come to make viewers (and readers) at least suspect that this may be the case. Romeo takes his leave just as Juliet's mother is about to enter.

It is always a good idea to go through the scene in chronological order

The situation does not improve with the entrance of Lady Capulet. She believes she is bringing news that will cheer her daughter after the death of her cousin Tybalt at Romeo's hand, but the news that Juliet is to marry Paris horrifies the young girl. Before Lady Capulet can get to the bottom of the matter, Capulet arrives. On hearing that Juliet refuses to marry Paris, he becomes extremely angry, calling her a 'young baggage' and a 'disobedient wretch'. He threatens her and speaks to her in a most cruel manner, adding to her misery.

Poor Juliet finds no support from her mother, despite pleading for her help and love: 'O, sweet my mother, cast me not away!' Lady Capulet is unmoved and, like Juliet's father, says that she will have nothing more to do with her. The scene could hardly be sadder nor Juliet's situation more pitiful, but there is more to come. The Nurse, who has been Juliet's companion and mother figure for many years, fails her too. She advises Juliet to marry Paris, calling him 'a lovely gentleman' and far better than Romeo. Juliet is completely alone. Romeo is gone, her parents have virtually disowned her, and now her last hope, the Nurse, has let her down. All of these events have happened in quick succession, which is most dramatic. Juliet's isolation is heartbreaking.

Words like 'heart-wrenching', 'poignant' and 'pitiful' support your view that this scene is a very sad one

The scene ends with Juliet's vow to take her own life if the Friar cannot help her to find a solution to her difficulties. It seems that she is now a truly tragic heroine as she says, 'If all else fail, myself have power to die.' This poignant, heart-wrenching scene touched me deeply and has stayed with me as one of the most powerful in the play.

QUESTION 2, SECTION 1, PAPER 2, JUNIOR CERT HL, 2003

Select a play you have studied.

(a) What did you learn about the world the characters of the play lived in? Support your answer by reference to the play. (20 marks)

(b) Did you like or dislike this world? Give reasons for your answer, making reference to the play. (10 marks)

Refer back to the notes on social setting. Not all of them will be relevant to *The Merchant of Venice,* but you should be able to select at least four to discuss for the twenty-mark question. This answer will focus on religion, the role of women, power and justice.

Sample Answer 1

2(a). What did you learn about the world the characters of the play lived in? Support your answer by reference to the play. (20)

The play I have studied for my Junior Certificate is William Shakespeare's The Merchant of Venice.

The world of the play is a fascinating one which gives us an insight into the mind-set of those who lived in Shakespeare's times. The aspects of the social setting about which I felt I learned most were religion, the role of women, power and justice.

The reason I was particularly struck by the way in which religion was dealt with in the play is that sectarianism is an issue which is as relevant now as it was four hundred years ago. However, this play seems to say that it is perfectly acceptable to openly and publicly detest people on the basis of their religion. Shylock says that he hates Antonio 'for he is a Christian' but this dislike is more than returned by Antonio who says, in response to Shylock's accusations of religious insults and general verbal

Name the play and the playwright in your opening sentence

Name the main aspects of social setting you plan to discuss in this answer

Try to link your points in order to make your answer flow well

**Quote to support
your points**

abuse, 'I am as like to call thee so again,/To spit on thee again, to
spurn thee too.'

In the final scenes of the play, Shylock loses everything: his
control of his fortune, his daughter and his religion. The other
characters openly delight in his downfall. Gratiano wishes aloud
that Shylock could have been hanged instead of being allowed to
convert:

> In christening shalt thou have two god-fathers:
> Had I been judge thou shouldst have had ten more,
> To bring thee to the gallows, not the font.

It is not only Shylock who is treated unfairly in The Merchant of
Venice, however. Portia may appear fortunate in that she has
wealth, wit and beauty, but she must still obey her late father's
wishes and marry the suitor who chooses the correct casket. She is
unhappy with this situation, saying to her friend, 'Is it not hard,
Nerissa, that I cannot choose one, nor refuse none?' In the world
of the play, women are expected to follow the wishes of the male
head of the household. Even a woman as clever as Portia is not
treated as an equal in this world: when she wants to appear in
Antonio's defence in court, she is forced to dress as a young man.
Even disguised as one 'of those bragging Jacks' she will be taken
more seriously than she would if she were to appear as herself.
She wins the case for Antonio by coming up with an angle none
of the men had thought of, but still she dare not reveal that she
is a woman.

It is clear that power in this play rests firmly in the hands of
wealthy, upper-class, Venetian, Christian men. Shylock may have
money but he is despised for being a Jew and considered an 'alien'
by the law of the land. Portia tells him that the court may take all
his money from him and that his life 'lies in the mercy/Of the duke
only'. Antonio is a citizen, while Shylock is not, therefore Shylock
is subject to harsher laws than a Venetian would be in the same
situation.

The Merchant of Venice is set in a world where the power of the law is most important. However, the law seems unjust. The court is prepared to allow Shylock to 'cut off the flesh' in order to satisfy the terms of his bond with Antonio, regardless of how barbaric this may be. Equally, nobody seems to see anything wrong with Antonio renegotiating Shylock's sentence and asking the duke to rule that 'He presently become a Christian' and that he dispose of his fortune as Antonio sees fit. The duke readily agrees and says that if Shylock does not do so he will be executed.

Sample Answer 2

2(b). Did you like or dislike this world? Give reasons for your answer, making reference to the play. (10)

This is a ten-mark question, so two or three paragraphs should be sufficient. You should deal with the points raised in the first half of this answer and give a personal response to each of them.

I would not like to live in the world of the play. It seems a cruel and unfair world where injustice and prejudice are rife.

While prejudice based on religious beliefs is prevalent nowadays, it is not generally something people are proud of. This is not the case in The Merchant of Venice. *Antonio, a respected member of Venetian society, is unrepentant when Shylock says, 'You call me misbeliever, cut-throat dog and spit upon my Jewish gaberdine.' I would most certainly not like to live in a world where such blatant prejudice was considered perfectly normal.*

I could not be happy in a world where people were discriminated against not just on the basis of religion, but also on the basis of gender. Portia has neither the power to choose her own husband nor the right to appear openly as an advocate in court. Power in the play rests with men alone.

The final reason I would not like to live in the world of the play

Part (b) of this answer requires you to reflect on what you discovered about the world of the play, so there is no need to write a conclusion here. Part (b) will serve as your conclusion, albeit a rather longer one than you might normally write

State your position in the opening sentence

Make sure that you show a personal response to each of the points you raise

Even in a short answer, you should try to link your points

is the way in which the law condones torture and death. The duke is prepared to allow Antonio to be mutilated and is equally prepared to threaten Shylock with death.

Although I enjoyed the play, I am very glad that I do not live in the world it depicts.

QUESTION 2, **SECTION 1, PAPER 2, JUNIOR CERT HL, 2007**

Name a play you have studied and state what you think is its main idea and/or message.
Explain how this main idea and/or message is communicated in the play. (30 marks)

Remember to confine yourself to one idea or message. Do not discuss a variety of themes, even if you are keen to show the examiner how much you know. All you will end up proving is that you do not know how to read a question properly.

Whatever message or idea you choose, it should be central to the play.

Make sure to discuss how Shakespeare communicates his message. That is an important part of this answer. A mere summary of key moments relating to the theme will not be sufficient.

Opinions differ, and others may not agree with your interpretation of the play. However, this is not important. What is important is your ability to argue convincingly. A well-thought-out, well-supported argument will get you a high grade. Refer back to the section on discursive writing (page 16) to find some techniques which might help.

Don't forget to name the play and playwright in the opening paragraph

The play I have studied for my Junior Certificate is William Shakespeare's Romeo and Juliet. I believe the main message in this play is that true love triumphs over all. This may seem a strange thing to say, given that both Romeo and Juliet die at the end of the play, but it seems clear to me that Shakespeare intended to convey the idea that true romantic love has the power to improve people and to make the world a better place.

There can be little doubt that Romeo is improved by true love. When we first meet him he is moody, unsociable and rather tiresome. His father says that he spends much of his time alone in his room where he closes the curtains and 'makes himself an artificial night'. He claims he is in love with a girl called Rosaline but we have reason enough to doubt that what he feels is genuine, sincere love. He mopes over Rosaline, calling her a woman of such incredible beauty that 'The all-seeing sun/Ne'er saw her match since first the world begun.' Romeo's overblown language and melodramatic behaviour are not convincing, and he does not come across as a particularly appealing character at this stage in the play.

Make sure that each point you make is supported by a key moment in the text with either a close reference or a quote. If you cannot remember the exact wording of the quote, it is better to paraphrase it than to guess and get it wrong

However, when Romeo meets Juliet, we see a different side of his character emerge. All his extravagant speeches end and he speaks of Juliet in simple, credible language. He realises now that up to this point he was more in love with the idea of being in love than he was with Rosaline. Seeing Juliet has made him ask himself, 'Did my heart love till now?' We may be initially inclined to wonder if this is merely Romeo switching his affections from one girl to another in a fickle way but he proves his love is real by remaining true to Juliet until the end. True love brings out the best in Romeo and makes him a hero worthy of our admiration.

Reference to language shows how Shakespeare gets his message across

The introduction to this answer stated that the power of love to improve people was important. Here we see how Romeo is improved by love

Romeo and Juliet's romantic view of love is not shared by the other characters. Juliet's parents regard love as an unnecessary component of marriage and are angry and bewildered when she refuses to marry the handsome, wealthy Paris. The Nurse agrees and suggests that Juliet should marry Paris, even though she is already married to Romeo. Romeo's friends are equally cynical about love. They make crude jokes about women and poke fun at love. Mercutio has little time for love and advises Romeo that 'If love be rough with you, be rough with love.' The Friar, too, is suspicious of passionate love and cautions Romeo that 'These violent delights have violent ends.' He feels that Romeo would be better to 'love moderately'. It is clear that both the hero and the heroine of this play are surrounded by those who see little merit in great, romantic passions. Romeo and Juliet have quite a task ahead of them if they are to prove that love does triumph.

Some critics have suggested that Romeo and Juliet never prove that love conquers all, but that their story actually shows what happens when young people disobey their parents and rashly enter into a passionate affair. After all, they argue, both Romeo and Juliet die, so is that not the message Shakespeare intends to convey?

I do not believe it is. The playwright ensures that Romeo and Juliet are attractive, appealing people. The scenes in which they profess their love for one another are beautiful and moving. At their final meeting, Juliet has a premonition of disaster when she says, 'O, thinkest thou we shall ever meet again?' We shiver along with Juliet as she says this and when she confesses her vision of Romeo 'As one dead in the bottom of a tomb'. Clearly, Shakespeare wants us to relate to the young lovers and to hope that they will succeed against the odds. His sympathetic characterisation puts us firmly on the side of Romeo and Juliet. We too want love to triumph.

But if the hero and heroine die, how can love be said to triumph? The answer is connected to the feud between the Montagues and the Capulets. We learned about the feud in the Prologue when we heard of the two families who 'From ancient grudge break to new mutiny'. Nothing has succeeded in ending the feud and this is the reason Romeo and Juliet have to keep their love secret. But with their deaths comes reconciliation between the families.

It is the Prince who, in the final scene, voices the main message of the play. He shows Capulet and Montague the bodies of their children and he tells them that 'heaven finds means to kill your

The answer is framed as an argument, so rhetorical questions are appropriate. Do not overuse them, however

Reference to characterisation shows how Shakespeare gets his message across

joys with love'. The grieving families vow to fight no more and peace is restored to Verona. In the end, Romeo and Juliet's deaths were not in vain.

This is, I feel, the main idea of the play. Love is powerful and love has the ability to bring about changes for the good, even if it also causes great sorrow. The play does not end on a pessimistic note. It ends by showing us that those who learn the message – that love conquers all – will go on to live better lives.

The conclusion refers back to the introduction and sums up the main points of the answer

UNSEEN POETRY

*The Unseen Poetry section of Paper 2 is worth **30 marks**.*

*You should spend about **25 minutes** on this section.*

In this section, you will be asked questions on a poem you have probably never seen before. Remember, the poem has been carefully chosen to be accessible to Junior Cert students, so the chances are that you will understand it fairly easily if you approach it calmly and sensibly.

Read the poem three times before attempting to answer the questions. You may wish to read the questions after the first or second reading, just to set you on the right track. Think of the poem as a comprehension piece: the answers are there in front of you; all you have to do is pick them out.

It is essential to read the questions very, very carefully. There may be two or three questions and there may be choices within the questions.

EXAM **FOCUS**   *There are many ways of interpreting a poem, and yours can be just as valid as anyone else's, provided you back up your points with quotes from the poem.*

When you are reading the poem, ask yourself a series of questions:

1. Does the **title** tell us anything? Is there an **introduction** to the poem? As in the drama section, this can be a great help.

2. **Who is speaking** in this poem? (It is worth noting the title and the poet's name; these may give you a hint. Remember, however, that a poet may be speaking from the point of view of a person of a different age or sex, or even as themselves when they were a child.)

8

3. Does the poet address the **subject** of the poem directly? Look out for use of the word 'you'. If the poet does this, it creates a sense of intimacy.

4. What is the poem about? In other words, what is the main **message** (theme) the poet is trying to get across to the reader?

5. What is the **mood** (tone) of the poem? Is it, for example, happy or sad, nostalgic or bitter? Try to imagine the poet reading the poem aloud. What tone of voice do you think he or she would use? This can help you work out the mood of the poem.

6. Does the mood of the poem **change** at all? Sometimes a poet may be angry at the start of a poem but calm and reflective by the end.

7. **Rhythm** – is the pace of the poem fast or slow? Does this tell us anything about the theme or the tone? (A slow rhythm is often associated with sadness.) What effect does the rhythm have? Does the rhythm vary? If so, why? Poems can have exciting moments between calm, reflective ones.

Read as much poetry as you can. You never know, you just might enjoy it ...

8. Look at the **images** in the poem. Are they effective? Do you like them?

Look out for metaphors. A storm may indicate a difficult relationship. A road may indicate a path in life or a choice the poet has to make.   EXAM **FOCUS**

---

9. Look at the **tense** or tenses used in the poem. The present tense can suggest immediacy or an unresolved issue. The past tense can indicate that the poet has come to terms with

the issue. Does the tense change at all? What does the tense change tell you? (Read the notes on tense change in 'The Lake Isle of Innisfree' in the Studied Poetry chapter (page 200) to see what effect such a change can have on the meaning of the poem.)

10. Think about the **literary terms** you learned when studying poetry in school. Start with sound: is there any alliteration, assonance, onomatopoeia, etc.? Underline these as you notice them.

11. What other **poetic techniques** does the poet use? Are metaphors, similes or symbols used? Are they effective? Do they help to create a picture in your mind?

12. What kind of **language** is used in the poem? Is it modern? Is it easy to understand? Is there slang? If so, why do you think it is used?

13. Do you **like** the poem?

This may seem like a lot to think about, and it certainly is if you wait until the day of the exam to do it for the first time. Get into the habit of doing it well before then. You may not be able to answer all these questions when reading a poem initially, but they will steer you along the path to better understanding the poem over time.

TYPICAL QUESTIONS AND HOW TO APPROACH THEM

While it is not possible to predict exactly what sort of questions will come up on the day of the exam, there are several that occur time and time again.

Theme

The main message of the poem. You may be asked, 'What does the poet think about …?' or, 'Choose a different title for this poem.'

Both of these questions are asking you the same thing: what is the poet's main message? If you had to sum it up in a few words, what would those words be?

Tone

The attitude of the poet towards the subject of the poem. You may be asked if you think the poem is happy or sad, or how the poet feels about the topic dealt with in the poem. Watch out for the words 'feeling', 'attitude' and 'mood' here. They can be a sign that the question is about tone.

Think of the tone of voice the poet would use if reading this poem aloud. Would the tone change as the poem progresses? Would some parts be read in a loud, excited voice and some in a quieter manner? The tone can change several times throughout the poem. If you notice changes as you are reading through it, jot them down on the page beside the relevant lines in the poem.

Style

This is a very common question and there is every likelihood that it will come up in your exam. Watch out for phrases such as, 'How does the poet give the impression that ...?' or, 'Do you think the poet captures the scene well?' You must refer to the language of the poem in your answer. This means that you must discuss the imagery, sounds, etc. This is your opportunity to use those key literary terms. It is important that you do so. (See below.) Start with sound: is there any alliteration, assonance, onomatopoeia, etc.? Remember, like drama, poetry is really meant to be read aloud and how the words sound is very important.

When you comment on a feature of style, be sure to use a verb to say what that feature does. This is vital. You may be asked if the poet describes something effectively. Don't forget to say why the description is effective. Look at Sample Answer 2 on the 2010 poem 'Cinders' (page 182) to see how this can be done.

EXAM **FOCUS** *Never refer to a poet by his or her first name only. It is acceptable to use the poet's surname on its own, or to use the full name. So, for example, you could say, 'Seamus Heaney is my favourite poet,' or 'Heaney is my favourite poet,' but you must never say, 'Seamus is my favourite poet.'*

Remember to read the instructions before the question closely. In some years candidates are asked to answer all the questions on a given poem and sometimes they are allowed to choose two out of three. You will waste time and lose marks if you do not do the right number of questions.

Characters or relationships

You may be asked what sort of person you think the poet or the subject of the poem is/was, based on what you have read. If you are asked, 'What impression do we get of this person?', you must use words to describe character. Try to use at least one 'character' word per paragraph.

Understanding

You may be asked to explain certain lines from the poem. Make sure you give a detailed answer here. Don't just simply paraphrase the lines; say why you came to that decision about them. Look at Sample Answer 2 on the 2006 poem 'Van Gogh's Yellow Chair' (page 186) to see how this can be done.

Your response to the poem

Did you like it? Why? Why not? You must explain yourself fully here. You are quite free to dislike the piece, but you must be prepared to back up your viewpoint with plenty of examples and quotations. It is generally far easier to say that you liked the poem and go through your list of literary terms, picking out those that appear in the poem and saying that you found them particularly striking or effective or evocative.

Bear in mind that this is a question on poetry. The examiners want to see a personal response based on a reasonably detailed analysis and evaluation of the poem.

Favourite image or images

You may be asked to select one or two images from the poem and explain your choice. Be sure to write out the images in full before explaining why you chose them.

Look at the question carefully. Does it suggest any things you 'may wish to consider'? This can be a great help when you are planning your answer.

EXAM **FOCUS**

QUESTION 1, SECTION 2, PAPER 2, JUNIOR CERT HL, 2010

Read the following poem by Roger McGough and answer the questions which follow.

Cinders

After the pantomime, carrying you back to the car   intimacy, past tense, calm
On the coldest night of the year
My coat, black leather, cracking in the wind.

Through the darkness we are guided by a star
It is the one the Good Fairy gave you
You clutch it tightly, your magic wand.

And I clutch you tightly for fear you blow away
For fear you grow up too soon and – suddenly,
I almost slip, so take it steady down the hill.

Hunched against the wind and hobbling
I could be mistaken for your grandfather
And sensing this, I hold you tighter still.
Knowing that I will never see you dressed for the Ball
Be on hand to warn you against Prince Charmings
And the happy ever afters of pantomime.

On reaching the car I put you into the baby seat
And fumble with straps I have yet to master
Thinking, if only there were more time. More time.

You are crying now. Where is your wand?
Oh no. I can't face going back for it
Let some kid find it in tomorrow's snow.

Waiting in the wings, the witching hour.
Already the car is changing. Smells sweet
Of ripening seed. We must go. Must go.

Roger McGough

*Answer **two** of the following questions. Each question is worth 15 marks.*

1. From your reading of the poem what do you learn about the relationship between the poet and his child? Base your answer on evidence from the poem.

2. Do you think the poet captures the scene well in this poem? Support your answer with reference to the poem.

3. Do you think this poem is sad or happy or a mixture of both? Explain your answer with reference to the poem.

Sample Answer 1

1. From your reading of the poem what do you learn about the relationship between the poet and his child? Base your answer on evidence from the poem. (15)

I think the poet has a very close relationship with his child. He addresses his daughter directly in the poem, using the word 'you' repeatedly. This creates a sense of intimacy and makes us feel as if we are listening in to a private conversation. McGough clearly feels very affectionate towards his daughter and makes several references to hugging her tightly to him. He is concerned about his daughter's happiness and expresses dismay when he realises why she is crying: 'Where is your wand?' Although he cannot face going back to get it, he is obviously sufficiently in tune with his child to know why she is upset.

Though the relationship is a good one, the poet is sad about certain aspects of it. He is older than most fathers of little girls: 'I could be mistaken for your grandfather', and he is worried that he won't see his daughter grow up. His sadness is apparent as he reflects on the fact that he will not live long enough to tell his daughter about the realities of life and warn her 'against Prince Charmings'. His wish that there could be 'more time' is a poignant one.

Like many fathers, the poet feels very protective of his little girl. He carries her back to the car, and holds her tightly 'for fear you blow away'. The words 'for fear' are repeated in the next line, emphasising the poet's concern for his daughter. His feeling of protectiveness is not just for the girl's well-being now, but also for her future happiness. He wishes he could protect her always, but life, he suggests, is not really about the 'happy ever afters of pantomime'.

From my reading of this poem, it is clear to me that the poet is a loving and concerned father who enjoys spending time with his little daughter and only wishes that he could always be around to take care of her.

Define the relationship immediately

Show how the poet uses language to convey his feelings

Quotes support each point

Link to next point, using 'Though the relationship is a good one …'

One point per paragraph

Work the quotes into the fabric of the sentence, rather than letting them stand alone

Brief conclusion. Remember, you should never introduce a new point in the conclusion

Sample Answer 2

2. Do you think the poet captures the scene well in this poem?
Support your answer with reference to the poem. (15)

This is a question on style, so concentrate on the language of the poem

I think the poet captures the scene very well in this poem. The physical descriptions of a father carrying his young daughter back to the car on a cold winter's night are both realistic and evocative. The repeated 'ack' sounds in the third line: 'My coat, black leather, cracking in the wind' mimic the sound I imagine the coat making as it snaps in the cold wind. He says that he and his daughter are 'guided by a star' and goes on to say it is the wand the little girl was given by the good fairy. This simply but effectively conjures up an image of the child proudly clutching the wand and holding it aloft as she is carried down the hill.

Don't just point out a feature of style; say what it does. In this case, link it back to the question by saying that it 'conjures up an image ...'

The poet unflinchingly faces up to the fact that he is an older father, and ruefully describes himself as 'Hunched against the wind and hobbling' as he picks his way carefully down the hill. This alliterative line, and the one which follows it in which he admits that he 'could be mistaken for your grandfather', draw us into the poet's moving but self-deprecating description of the scene. He tells us that he 'fumbles with the straps' of the baby seat. This little detail adds to the poignancy and gives us the impression that there is much about practically parenting the little girl that causes him difficulties. It is easy to picture a frustrated McGough struggling with the nylon straps in the dark as the child cries for the lost wand.

Use poetic terminology throughout the answer

Again, say what this image does. It makes it 'easy to picture' the father. Refers to the question

I was struck by the way in which the poet blends the world of the pantomime and the real world to create a scene which is both charming and sweetly sad. The little girl is probably lost in the story of the pantomime she has just seen, and McGough's reflection that he will never see his daughter 'dressed for the Ball', nor will he be 'on hand to warn you against Prince Charmings' effectively captures the sad reality of the scene. Here he is, with his small daughter in his arms, clutching her tightly, and yet fully

In each paragraph, reflect the wording of the question by mentioning the way in which the scene is created

aware that he cannot hold her for ever. The simple but descriptive language and the poet's bittersweet thoughts really bring the scene to life for me.

Brief conclusion, referring to the question

Sample Answer 3

3. Do you think this poem is sad or happy or a mixture of both? Explain your answer with reference to the poem. (15)

As was stated in the drama section, if you are presented with a question inviting you to discuss both options in the answer, you should do so. For example, this question clearly paves the way for you to discuss both the happy and the sad aspects of the poem. Remember, you don't have to say that the poem contains equal amounts of happiness and sadness, just that it contains elements of both.

I think that this poem is both happy and sad. It opens on a positive note and presents us with the heart-warming image of the poet carrying his beloved daughter back to the car after a night out together at the pantomime. Roger McGough is a caring father who holds his little girl as tightly as she holds her magic wand. She is precious to him and he clutches her to him 'for fear you blow away'. This concern for his child is touching but even in this early part of the poem there is a note of sadness in the poet's fear that his daughter will 'grow up too soon'.

Words like 'positive' and 'heart-warming' reinforce the idea that this is a happy image

The sadness in the poem centres on the poet's realisation that – as he is an older father – he will not always be there for his little girl, and he will not be around to see her 'dressed for the Ball'. This story will not end in 'happy ever afters'.

The answer moves through the poem, discussing the changes of mood as the poem progresses

The mood of the poem becomes less happy and more sad as the poet and his daughter reach the car. He struggles to tie the straps of the car seat and admits that he has 'yet to master' them. This could be a symbol for all the things he needs to learn about raising his little girl and the lack of time he has in which to do this. The

Each paragraph reflects the question asked

poet's plaintive wish for 'More time' is emphasised by the repetition of this phrase at the end of the sixth stanza. The child is crying now as she has lost her wand and this adds to the feeling of sadness.

The conclusion reflects the point made in the opening sentence and ties the answer up neatly

Although the poem ends on a melancholy note, with the poet keenly aware that his time with his daughter is limited, his love for her and his concern for her future is a constant throughout the poem. For this reason, I find the poem to be a blend of happiness and sadness.

QUESTION 1, SECTION 2, PAPER 2, JUNIOR CERT HL, 2006

Read the following poem (in edited form) by Mark Roper and answer the questions which follow.

Van Gogh's Yellow Chair

I would love to sit
in the yellow chair
in the painting

when a shadow lies
like a shy animal
in a corner

and the day's air
is like water in which
small noises swim

I would sit there
safe from harm
safe from all surprise.

Beyond the frame
on every side
the outside world

would open wide
but I'd have crossed
the great divide

so long as I never
rose from
that yellow chair.

Mark Roper

*Answer **two** of the following questions. Each question is worth 15 marks.*

1. *'I would love to sit*
   in the yellow chair
   in the painting ...'

What is so appealing about Van Gogh's yellow chair, according to the speaker? Explain your answer with reference to the poem.

2. *In your own words explain what is being said in the last three stanzas.*

3. *What is your favourite image from the poem? Explain your choice.*

Sample Answer 1

1. 'I would love to sit
   in the yellow chair
   in the painting ...'
What is so appealing about Van Gogh's yellow chair, according to the speaker? Explain your answer with reference to the poem. (15)

I think that the speaker is drawn to the yellow chair because it offers him a chance to escape to a more attractive world. Everything about the chair and the room in which it sits is portrayed in a positive way. The yellow colour of the chair evokes

The main point is made in the opening sentence

This question asked what is appealing about the yellow chair, so words like 'positive', 'happiness' and 'peace' are used to reinforce the idea that each point proves how appealing the chair is

feelings of warmth, sun and happiness. If the speaker were to sit in this chair, he could enjoy the calm atmosphere of his surroundings. There, all is peace. A shadow 'lies/like a small animal in a corner' and sounds are muffled to 'small noises' by air which is 'like water'.

The poet seems to view the real world as a hostile place because, in the fourth stanza, he says that if he were to sit in the yellow chair he would be 'safe from harm'. He would also be 'safe from all surprise'. The repetition of the word 'safe' shows the importance the poet attaches to the chair as an imaginary place of sanctuary.

It is always a good idea to comment on the language in the poem. For example, in the second paragraph of this answer, the repetition of the word 'safe' is highlighted

The idea of being able to see the 'outside world' but not having to be a part of it is, I feel, what the speaker particularly likes about the notion of sitting in the yellow chair. If he were to escape into this world he would be in a better place. It would be the world of art and imagination and from there he would be able to see things from a different perspective. He would have 'crossed/the great divide'. Nothing would bother him as long as he stayed there. It is easy to see, when you look at it this way, why the poet says that he would 'love/to sit in the yellow chair in the painting'.

Sample Answer 2

2. In your own words explain what is being said in the last three stanzas. (15)

The key word in this question is 'explain'. If you just paraphrase the last three stanzas, you will get a very low grade

The last three stanzas of this poem show the speaker's desire to escape from this world into a very different one.

The speaker tells us that if he somehow managed to achieve his desire and become part of the painting, then he would be apart from 'the outside world'. He talks of a 'great divide' between the real world and the world of art. The frame of the painting resembles a fence or a wall, separating him from the world and keeping him from harm. I was struck by the description of the outside world opening wide, like a huge mouth that would devour *the speaker, or like a void in which he would be lost for ever. The idea of his feeling safer in the painting is reinforced by the words 'so long'. Everything would be fine 'so long as I never/rose from/that yellow chair'. If he did rise, all this security and tranquillity would vanish.*

There is also a sense of the world of art allowing us to see our own world in a new way. There is an interesting reversal of the normal order of things in this poem. Usually, we look at paintings, but the speaker wants to become part of the painting, and to look out at the real world from a different perspective. I think he is saying that if we lose ourselves in art, if we allow ourselves to become totally absorbed by it, we will have a new view of the world 'Beyond the frame'.

Finally, I believe that the last three stanzas show us how we should not be limited and unimaginative in our thinking. Paintings can offer us doorways into other worlds and open up all sorts of creative and imaginative options. We can lose ourselves in a work of art and in a world of art. We can stretch our minds and visualise ourselves as part of a painting, rather than just standing and admiring it in a practical, down-to-earth way.

As this is a fifteen-mark question, try to make three separate points. Give each point its own paragraph

Quote to support points being made. Weave the quotes into the fabric of the sentence if possible

Personal response is appropriate here. You are required to explore the meaning behind the words

Sample Answer 3

3. What is your favourite image from the poem? Explain your choice. (15)

It can be difficult to write more than a couple of paragraphs on a question about one image. Don't write more just for the sake of it. Quality is more important than quantity, and if you ramble or introduce irrelevant points, you will lose marks.

My favourite image in the poem is 'a shadow lies/like a shy animal/in the corner'. I like this simile because it seems to bring the painting to life. Others may look at the painting and see it as something inanimate and unchanging, but the speaker sees it as

Make sure to quote the image in full

Define the image. It is a simile

something real and vital. For him, the shadow in the corner is not simply paint on canvas; it is alive and might, like a shy animal, slip away at any moment.

Explain why you liked the image

The image also appeals to me because it seemed to give the poem a friendly feeling. Shadows can be frightening as they may hide dangers, but this shadow is like a 'shy animal'. Far from being a threat, it is portrayed as something timid and easily frightened. This rather sweet image adds to the welcoming, comforting atmosphere of the world of 'the yellow chair'. Having an animal curled up at your feet or in the corner is relaxing and soothing, and the poet's decision to compare the shadow to a 'shy animal' reinforces the notion of this magical place as being somewhere 'safe from harm/safe from all surprise'. It is a very positive image and very evocative of an idyllic place. I think this charming and unusual simile will stay with me for a long time to come.

Use verbs to say what the image does: 'brings the painting to life' ... 'adds to the welcoming, comforting atmosphere', etc.

Say what the image does in terms of the poem as a whole

STUDIED POETRY

*The Studied Poetry section of Paper 2 is worth **30 marks**.*

*You should spend about **25 minutes** on this section.*

In the Studied Poetry section of Paper 2, you will be asked to answer a question on a poet, poem or poems you have covered in class.

Most students will have studied anywhere between six and twelve poems in some detail in the years leading up to the Junior Cert. It is important to have all these poems to hand, ideally in a separate folder, so that you can arrange them in order of theme. The more poems you have studied, the greater choice you will have when it comes to selecting which question you will answer.

The poems you have studied will deal with a number of different themes. When you are revising your poems, it is a good idea to write beside each one how many different themes you can see. For example, Wendy Cope's 'Tich Miller' deals with childhood, school, isolation, loneliness, revenge and death. It is also a very good portrait of a person.

You must be able to show that you understand the technical aspects of the poetry. This means using key literary terms such as 'tone', 'theme' and 'metaphor'.

Be positive on exam day. You know more than you give yourself credit for

While the questions asked are quite general, you need to know your chosen poems very well and in great detail. It is generally easier to learn a whole poem by heart than to learn a few quotes here and there. The rhyme and the rhythm of poetry can be a great help here.

9

PREPARING FOR THE STUDIED POETRY QUESTION

You should study each of your chosen poems closely. You will be expected to be capable of commenting on everything from the theme to the title. If you only have a vague understanding of the poems, you will not get a high mark in this section.

It is important to be able to speak at some length about the work of an individual poet and to know two or three poems by that poet in great detail.

You may have your studied poems in different copy books, text books or folders. This is an inefficient system and makes it difficult for you to see at a glance how many poems you have studied. Organise the poems into a separate folder as soon as you can. This may mean printing out or copying out the poems and the notes again, but this is not a bad thing as reproducing material is a valuable revision exercise and will help you to learn the poems off by heart.

When learning your poems, look at the rhyme scheme. Do the last words in every second line rhyme, for example? Knowing the rhyme scheme can help you learn the poems by heart.

EXAM **FOCUS**

TYPES OF QUESTION

There are four main types of question in the Junior Cert exam:

1. A question which deals with a particular **theme**
    (love, war, family, etc.)

2. A question which asks you to **compare** and/or **contrast** two poems which deal with the same theme in different ways

3. A question which asks for your **personal response** to a poem or poems you have studied

4. A question about a particular **poet** you have studied

Remember, the examiner will have no idea which poems you have studied, so when you are writing your answer **it is essential that you name the chosen poems and poets at the outset**.

Past questions have asked the following:

- Discuss the ways in which two poems you have studied deal with a similar theme. Say which poem you preferred and why

- Select a poem which celebrates a person, place or thing. Discuss the theme and the way in which the sense of celebration is created.

- Discuss the work of your favourite poet.

- Show how the imagery of a poem you have selected helps your understanding of the theme.

- Choose a poem which has a special meaning for you and explain how the poet used language and imagery in a way which helped you to identify with the theme.

- Write in detail about a poem which deals with a particular theme such as love, war, memories, old age, hopes, childhood, etc.

EXAM **FOCUS**   *Keep your quotes short and relevant.*

WRITING YOUR ANSWER

Read the question very carefully. See how many parts there are to the question and make sure you take note of the marks allotted to each part.

Paraphrase the question; in other words, try to ask yourself exactly what you are being asked to do and think how you would explain the question to a friend.

Thirty-mark questions should be written in essay form. If you are answering a thirty-mark question, you should aim to write around six paragraphs (an introduction, four main paragraphs and a conclusion). This will mean that, for most people, the essay will fill approximately two pages of the answer book.

It is vital to name the poet and the poem in the opening sentence. If you do not do this, you will lose marks.

Your introduction should reflect the wording of the question.

Say 'In my opinion' or 'I think' but not both together.   EXAM **FOCUS**
They mean the same thing.

Plan your answer carefully and decide the order in which you are going to make your points. As this is an essay, you will need to ensure that there is a beginning, a middle and an end. Link your paragraphs whenever it is possible to do so. A fluid, well-constructed essay will get you an A grade. A series of disconnected points, no matter how valid they are, will not.

Avoid summarising the poems. You will not be given marks for doing this.

Remember that you must use quotations and they must be linked to the answer. Do not simply leave them hanging in the middle of the answer, unexplained. Also, remember that although quotes are important, they must not form the body of your answer. They support your point, but they do not replace it. Some students believe that if they pad out their answer with lots of quotes, they will get high marks. They will not. Rote learning is all well and good, but it is not a substitute for analysis and understanding.

Make sure you can spell the name of the poet and the poem. Check   EXAM **FOCUS**
which words in the poem's title begin with a capital letter.

VOCABULARY

Below is a list of words you may find helpful when planning your answer:

- absorbing (occupies all your attention)
- attention-grabbing
- compelling (demands your attention)
- effective
- engrossing (absorbing)
- enjoyable
- evocative (stirs up an emotional response in you)
- exciting
- fascinating
- gripping
- interesting
- intriguing (really engages your interest)
- moving
- poignant (deeply and painfully affecting)
- remarkable
- riveting (holds your attention)
- stimulating
- striking
- thought-provoking

EXAM **FOCUS** *Try to use accurate words rather than vague ones like 'good' or 'nice'. Learn the spellings of the words given in this section.*

Think about the following verbs when you are explaining why you find an image effective:

- amuses
- captures
- creates
- emphasises
- engages
- evokes (calls to mind or suggests)
- fascinates
- moves

- personalises
- persuades
- proves
- provokes
- stirs
- suggests

Link words and phrases

- also
- both poems/poets
- conversely
- differs from
- each poem
- however
- in contrast
- in the same manner
- in the same way
- just as
- likewise
- on the contrary
- similarly
- this is different from
- whereas
- while

Between now and the exam, you should practise writing answers to the types of question given in this chapter.

EXAM **FOCUS**

KEY LITERARY TERMS

Alliteration – The repetition of initial consonant sounds, for example: 'I hear lake water lapping with low sounds by the shore.' Alliteration can help to create a mood; repeated 's' sounds, for example, can make a line sound calm and soothing.

Allusion – A reference to another writer or to something else which is not really part of the main body of the poem. For example, in 'Dulce et Decorum est' Wilfred Owen alludes to the work of the poet Horace when he quotes the Latin words in the title and at the end of the poem.

Assonance – The repetition of vowel sounds. In this verse from Edgar Allen Poe's poem 'The Bells', the examples of assonance have been underlined. Assonance is best appreciated when the poem is read aloud, although this is not possible in an exam situation, of course.

Hear the mellow wedding bells – Golden bells!
What a world of happiness their harmony foretells!
Through the balmy air of night
How they ring out their delight!
From the molten-golden notes,
And all in tune,
What a liquid ditty floats
To the turtle-dove that listens, while she gloats
On the moon!

Couplet – Two successive lines of poetry which have the same rhythm and rhyme. These two lines often contain a complete thought. All of Shakespeare's sonnets end with a couplet. Here is an example from Shakespeare's 'Shall I Compare Thee':

So long as men can breathe, or eyes can see,
So long lives this, and this gives life to thee.

Enjambment – When a sentence continues into the next line of the poem without any punctuation mark. Enjambment is often used to suggest fast action or movement. Enjambment is sometimes called a 'run-on line'.

Imagery – Words used which create a vivid picture in your mind.

Metaphor – A comparison in which the words 'like' or 'as' are not used. 'My love is a red, red rose.' A metaphor is generally considered to be stronger than a simile.

Onomatopoeia – When a word sounds like its meaning. Examples of onomatopoeia are: ***squelch, thud, slap, cackle, buzz, hiss.***

EXAM **FOCUS** *This can appear to be a difficult word to spell, but if you break it up, it's easy. ONO-MATO-POEIA. Think of the spelling of 'poem' when you are learning the last piece of the word. There is a 'poe' in 'poem' and in the 'poeia' part of 'onomatopoeia'.*

Repetition – Repeated words or phrases can emphasise the idea which the poet is exploring. Repetition often occurs near the end of the poem and can help to bring it to a pleasing close as well as adding to the rhythm. An example of repetition used in this way can be seen in Shakespeare's 'Shall I Compare Thee':

So long as men can breathe, or eyes can see,
So long lives this, and this gives life to thee.

The repetition here stresses the notion that the poet's love will last forever.

Simile – A comparison in which the words 'like' or 'as' are used. 'My love is like a red, red rose.'

Symbol – A word which stands for something more than the object to which it refers. For example, a rose may be a symbol of love and a dove may be a symbol of peace.

Theme – The main message of the poem, what the poem is about. It is not the story of the poem. For example, the theme of Wilfred Owen's 'Dulce et Decorum est' is that there is neither honour nor nobility in dying for your country.

Tone – The poet's mood or attitude towards the subject of the poem.

SELECTED POEMS – AN INTRODUCTION

There is no list of prescribed poems for Junior Certificate English. Teachers are free to choose any poems they wish. Certain poems tend to be favourites with many teachers, and for good reasons. The themes and the language in these poems make them suitable for study at junior cycle level, and these poems are also frequently included in textbooks.

EXAM **FOCUS**   *Check with your classmates to make sure you have the same list of poems. You may have missed one or two.*

In the following pages there are notes on several poems which cover some of the themes dealt with in Junior Cert. You may or may not have studied them in school. If you have, my notes can be a useful addition to those given to you by your teacher. If not, don't worry. They are just examples of the types of poem frequently covered. Your teacher will have covered plenty of poems in class which will enable you to answer any question in the exam.

It is important to note that you must deal with the aspects of language in the poems as well as the themes. In other words, you must say **how** the poet gets his or her message across and **what effect** this has on you as a reader. Support each point you make with a suitable quote from the poem. Look at the extract below from the notes on 'The Lake Isle of Innisfree'.

Point out that the poet switches to the present tense, and say that this makes him appear deeply involved with his vision of the isle

In this stanza, Yeats becomes so involved with the idea of this peaceful paradise that the future tense is abandoned and he uses the present tense instead. It is almost as if, by thinking and writing about Innisfree, he imagines himself there at that moment. He tells us that 'peace comes dropping slow' and 'midnight's all a-glimmer'. He moves through each stage of the

Give examples of the imagery used and say that this brings Yeats' vision to life and creates a peaceful, calm atmosphere

day, bringing his vision to life for us with his vivid descriptions and beautiful imagery. In the morning, the mist is like veils thrown over the lake; at noon, the purple heather blazes under the sun; the evening is full of the whirr of the linnet's wings (the linnet is a small songbird), and at night the stars fill the sky: 'midnight's all a-glimmer'. The sounds in this stanza are soft and slow, creating a sense of peace and calm.

In other words: feature of style + verb saying what the feature does = good point.

The Lake Isle of Innisfree

I will arise and go now, and go to Innisfree,
And a small cabin build there, of clay and wattles made;
Nine bean rows will I have there, a hive for the honeybee,
And live alone in the bee-loud glade.

And I shall have some peace there, for peace comes dropping slow,
Dropping from the veils of the morning to where the cricket sings;
There midnight's all a-glimmer, and noon a purple glow,
And evening full of the linnet's wings.

I will arise and go now, for always night and day
I hear lake water lapping with low sounds by the shore;
While I stand on the roadway, or on the pavements grey,
I hear it in the deep heart's core.

W.B. Yeats

Glossary

Wattles – wooden poles, intertwined with thin branches to form a wall or roof.

Glimmer – flicker of light (here used to mean the twinkle of stars).

Linnet – a small songbird, once commonly kept as a cage bird because of its beautiful singing.

Background

Yeats wrote this poem in 1888 when he was a young man living in London. He was lonely and homesick for Ireland at the time. Looking in a shop window, he saw a toy fountain and the sound of the water reminded him of lake water. Inspired by this, he wrote 'The Lake Isle of Innisfree'.

Note

Some students refer to the name of the island – Innisfree – as having something to do with freedom. This is not the case. 'Innisfree' is an Anglicisation of 'Inis Fraoch', which means 'Island of Heather'.

Analysis

Stanza One

The poem opens very formally with the words 'I will arise and go now, and go to Innisfree'. It has been pointed out that these words echo those of the prodigal son in the Bible when he says, 'I will arise and go to my father.' These biblical overtones reinforce the idea of Innisfree being an almost holy place and bring to mind the prodigal son's sense of relief when he resolved to leave his chaotic, unhappy life and return to his childhood home – a place of serenity and simplicity.

The poet goes on to describe the life he will lead on the island. He will be completely self-sufficient, having 'nine bean rows' and 'a hive for the honeybee'. The poet's vision is of a romantic, idyllic, timeless way of life. Yeats imagines living in peace and solitude; he says he will 'live alone in the bee-loud glade'. The only sounds will be of nature. It seems that Yeats is rejecting the hustle and bustle of the modern world. The details in the poem give it a timeless quality; there is no hint of the modern world in Yeats' vision.

Stanza Two

In this stanza, Yeats becomes so involved with the idea of this peaceful paradise that the future tense is abandoned and he uses the present tense instead. It is almost as if, by thinking and writing about Innisfree, he imagines himself there at that moment. He tells us that 'peace comes dropping slow' and 'midnight's all a-glimmer'. He moves through each stage of the day, bringing his vision to life for us with his vivid descriptions and imagery. In the morning, the mist is like veils thrown over the lake; at noon, the purple heather blazes under the sun; the evening is full of the whirr of the linnet's wings (the linnet is a small songbird) and at night, the stars fill the sky: 'midnight's all a-glimmer'. The sounds in this stanza are soft and slow, creating a sense of peace and calm.

Stanza Three

Yeats brings us back to the opening lines in this stanza, beginning again with the words 'I will arise and go'. The solemnity is reinforced and emphasised by this repetition, as is the strength of his longing. The alliteration and assonance in the line, 'I hear lake water lapping with low sounds by the shore' emphasise the tranquillity of the scene Yeats is describing. The broad vowels in this line slow the movement of the poem. In contrast to this timeless, magical, colourful place, we are reminded of Yeats' reality at the time of writing: 'While I stand on the roadway, or on the pavements grey'. The colourless grey of the pavements seems dreary and depressing and we can empathise with Yeats' yearning for the Lake Isle of Innisfree, a yearning he feels in 'the deep heart's core'. The last line is monosyllabic, which drives home the simple strength of the message.

Themes

- The poet's discontent, which leads him to imagine this perfect place
- A longing to go back to nature and live a self-sufficient life
- The search for peace, wisdom and truth

This poem could be used to answer a question on:

- Wishes or thoughts
- An interesting place
- Sound effects or musical qualities
- A poem I would recommend
- A poem which captures the imagination
- Interesting imagery

The Wild Swans at Coole

The trees are in their autumn beauty,
The woodland paths are dry,
Under the October twilight the water
Mirrors a still sky;
Upon the brimming water among the stones
Are nine-and-fifty swans.

The nineteenth autumn has come upon me
Since I first made my count;
I saw, before I had well finished,
All suddenly mount
And scatter wheeling in great broken rings
Upon their clamorous wings.

I have looked upon those brilliant creatures,
And now my heart is sore.
All's changed since I, hearing at twilight,
The first time on this shore,
The bell-beat of their wings above my head,
Trod with a lighter tread.

Unwearied still, lover by lover,
They paddle in the cold
Companionable streams or climb the air;
Their hearts have not grown old;
Passion or conquest, wander where they will,
Attend upon them still.

But now they drift on the still water,
Mysterious, beautiful;
Among what rushes will they build,
By what lake's edge or pool
Delight men's eyes when I awake some day
To find they have flown away?

W.B. Yeats

Background

Yeats wrote this poem in 1916, when he was 51 years of age. Coole Park in Co. Galway was the home of Lady Augusta Gregory, Yeats' friend and patron. (A patron is a wealthy or influential supporter of an artist or writer.) In the poem, he reflects on how his life has changed since he was a younger man and walked 'with a lighter tread'.

In 1916, Yeats' love, Maud Gonne, was widowed. Her husband, Major John McBride, had been executed by the British for his part in the Easter Rising. Maud Gonne went to France to work as a nurse with the war wounded and Yeats followed her to propose marriage once again. Once again she refused. In 1917, Yeats married Georgiana Hyde-Lees and moved into Thoor Ballylee, a house near Coole Park.

Analysis

Stanza One

Yeats begins the poem by describing the beauty of Coole Park in the autumn. Details such as the brimming water and the dry woodland paths bring this peaceful scene to life. The brimming water of the lake contrasts with the dry paths. It is as if the lake and its occupants represent life and growth, while the land – where Yeats stands – is barren. Autumn is linked with slowing down and dying. Does Yeats feel that, at 51, he is reaching the autumn years of his life? The swans are counted; there are 'nine-and-fifty' of them. Swans mate for life, so why is there an odd number? Is one of them, like Yeats, alone? The repeated 'm', 's' and 'l' sounds in this stanza emphasise the sense of peace and quiet. The tone of this stanza is quite detached. The descriptions are given without any obvious emotion.

Stanza Two

In the second stanza, Yeats becomes far more personal as he recalls that it is nineteen years since he first counted these swans. Although logic tells us that these are unlikely to be the same swans, we suspend disbelief and accept that this is just an artistic construct. Suddenly, before Yeats can finish his counting, all the swans rise into the air. The run-on lines suggest movement and reflect the swans' flight. The onomatopoeic word 'clamorous' effectively captures the clapping and beating of the swans' wings as they soar into the air. They form a ring – a symbol of eternity – and perhaps this reminds Yeats that while he might change, the swans remain the same, and even make the same patterns in the sky every year.

Stanza Three

The poet reflects how everything in his life has changed since he first looked at the swans on this lake. He is not as young or as carefree as he was when he 'Trod with a lighter tread'. His 'heart is sore' as he thinks of the loss of his youth and of his failed romances. The description of the swans' wings in flight, 'The bell-beat of their wings' is particularly effective here. The alliteration in 'bell-beat' captures and reinforces the steady beat of the birds' huge wings as they fly above his head.

Stanza Four

There is a note of envy in the fourth stanza as Yeats watches the birds, 'Unwearied still, lover by lover,' paddling together in the 'Companionable streams'. The streams may be cold, but the swans have one another. They are united, and time does not seem to touch them: 'Their hearts have not grown old'. Wherever they go, 'Passion or conquest' are with them. This seems to be in contrast to Yeats' own life. He implies that he is old and tired and heartbroken. The swans can swim in the 'brimming' water and fly in the air, but Yeats is limited to the dry woodland paths.

Stanza Five

The poem ends with Yeats wondering where the swans will go next to 'Delight men's eyes'. Perhaps he means that they, unchanged, will continue to bring pleasure to others who stand as he does now, watching them glide once more on the still water. The poem is set in autumn, and winter will inevitably follow for the poet. The swans seem untouched by everything and will continue to 'drift on the still water'. Yeats may be thinking of his creative life or his love life, or both, when he reflects on the changes that time has wrought. The swans are unchanging, content, almost immortal. He is none of these things.

Theme

*   The passage of time and the loss of youth, creative
    vision and love

This poem could be used to answer a question on:

*   Old age
*   A poem I would recommend
*   A poem which captures the imagination
*   Sound effects or musical qualities
*   Interesting imagery
*   A poem which deals with an important issue
    (see 'Theme', page 197)

Shall I Compare Thee?

Shall I compare thee to a Summer's day?
Thou art more lovely and more temperate:
Rough winds do shake the darling buds of May,
And Summer's lease hath all too short a date:
Sometime too hot the eye of heaven shines,
And oft' is his gold complexion dimm'd;
And every fair from fair sometime declines,
By chance or nature's changing course untrimm'd:
But thy eternal Summer shall not fade
Nor lose possession of that fair thou owest;
Nor shall Death brag thou wanderest in his shade,
When in eternal lines to time thou growest:

So long as men can breathe, or eyes can see,
So long lives this, and this gives life to thee.

William Shakespeare

Analysis

In the opening line of this sonnet, Shakespeare asks if he should compare his loved one to a summer's day. The obvious answer would seem to be that he should, but in fact he does not. He goes on to say that his beloved is more lovely and more temperate (less extreme/milder) than such a beautiful day. This sets the tone for the first two quatrains (four lines) in which the poet explains why summer does not match up to his beloved. Note that the poet is speaking directly to his beloved in the sonnet. This adds a sense of intimacy to the poem.

The poet tells us that even in May the buds can be shaken by 'rough winds'. He also points out that summer does not last long. It has 'all too short a date'. Sometimes the sun burns too brightly and it is too hot, and at other times the 'gold complexion' of the sun is 'dimm'd' or hidden by clouds. Everything that is fair or beautiful can fade, either by accident – 'chance' – or the changing seasons: 'nature's changing course'. The beauty of summer fades into autumn each year. For this reason, the poet does not want to compare his loved one to something so transient and imperfect as a summer's day.

This is an interesting reversal of the normal expectations which might be raised by the question the poet asks in the first line. We could reasonably expect the poet, having asked such a question, to justify why he might say that his beloved is every bit as lovely as a summer's day. But this is not the case. Instead, he holds the summer's day up to the harsh light of criticism, and finds it wanting – compared to the object of his affections. This shows us the strength of feeling Shakespeare has for his beloved. Normally, when a poet uses metaphors, similes or analogies, the purpose is to show how the subject of the poem matches up to the object to which they are compared. Here, it is the other way around. Such a reversal makes us sit up and take notice in a way we might not to more clichéd praise of an adored object.

In the third quatrain, Shakespeare addresses his beloved again. He has told us why the summer cannot compare to his loved one, and now he explains why his beloved's beauty is more long-lasting. The use of the word 'But' signals this change in the poem. The poet says that the loved one's beauty will not fade or be forgotten because it will be immortalised in this poem. Even when his loved one dies, Death will not be able to boast that he has control now. Shakespeare's beloved will live on in the lines he has written and will not fade in death but will continue to grow because of his sonnet. The lines will be 'eternal' and in them the loveliness which Shakespeare treasures will be preserved for all time.

The sonnet ends with a couplet (two lines) in which Shakespeare makes the claim that as long as there are people on earth, his loved one's beauty will live. He says that the poem will live as long as there are people to read it, and because of that his beloved will live on too and will be given eternal life by the sonnet.

The repetition of the words 'So long' in both lines and 'this' in the final line emphasise the theme of the poem as well as giving a pleasing end to the sonnet.

A Shakespearean sonnet consists of fourteen lines, each containing ten syllables and written in **iambic pentameter**. Iambic pentameter means that the poem has a fixed rhythm in which an unstressed syllable is followed by a stressed syllable. This is repeated five times in each line, giving a total of ten syllables per line.

If we look at the final couplet of this sonnet, for example, we can see this rhythm clearly. Only the stressed syllables are underlined.

So long as men can breathe, or eyes can see,
So long lives this, and this gives life to thee.

The iambic pentameter makes the poem easier to remember, but also makes the sentiments expressed seem more definite and convincing than they might appear in a poem with a looser rhythm or rhyme scheme.

Themes

- Love

The love expressed in this poem is simply yet movingly expressed. The language is straightforward and each line is self-contained. This can be seen in the number of punctuation marks: most lines end with one.

- The passing of time/fleeting nature of beauty

This poem is about the transience of life and of beauty. As long as both are linked to physical beings, they will pass away. However, if they are captured in poetry, they can live for ever.

This poem could be used to answer a question on:
- Love
- A poem I would recommend
- Interesting imagery

Tich Miller

Tich Miller wore glasses
with elastoplast-pink frames
and had one foot three sizes larger than the other.

When they picked teams for outdoor games
she and I were always the last two
left standing by the wire-mesh fence.

We avoided one another's eyes
stooping, perhaps, to re-tie a shoe-lace
or affecting interest in the flight

of some fortunate bird, and pretended
not to hear the urgent conference:
'Have Tubby!' 'No, no, have Tich!'

Usually they chose me, the lesser dud
and she lolloped, unselected,
to the back of the other team.

At eleven we went to different schools.
In time I learned to get my own back,
sneering at hockey players who couldn't spell.

Tich died when she was twelve.

Wendy Cope

Analysis

This poem deals with the cruelty of schoolchildren and the way in which young people can feel isolated from their peers.

The opening lines introduce Tich immediately. The use of her name, as opposed to simply calling her 'a girl in my class', makes us feel connected with the subject of the poem and brings a note of reality to the topic. We know the girl's name, and this brings her to life for us, in a way. She is not just a statistic or an anonymous sufferer of bullying or isolation: she is a real girl.

Tich is described as wearing glasses in a sickly colour of pink: the colour of Elastoplast. There is nothing attractive about this image and we may well wonder at this stage about the poet's intentions. Is she setting out to mock Tich? She is not, although others do. Tich's unfortunate appearance is highlighted again in the third line when we learn that one of her feet was three sizes larger than the other. There is something almost humorous about this image, but not quite. The poet's language is simple and stark and we are faced with the tragicomedy of a young girl who is almost clownish, but whose plight arouses our sympathy rather than our laughter. The simplicity of the language throughout the poem reflects the simplicity of the language and thought process of young children, while also forcing us to face the issues being dealt with. There is no flowery language, no euphemisms to hide the harsh reality.

In the second stanza, the poet links herself to Tich. When it came time to choose team members for games, the poet and Tich were always left until last. The mention of the 'wire-mesh fence' makes us think of prison, or a cage. The pair are trapped in their bodies and trapped in their shared plight. They cannot escape the embarrassment which befalls them week in, week out. The use of the word 'always' suggests that this ritual humiliation was a common occurrence.

Although Tich and the poet are united in their distress, they are not closer because of it. They avoid making eye contact with one another and pretend to tie a shoelace which did not need to be re-tied rather than talk to one another. Perhaps they want to avoid facing the fact that they are both rejected by their classmates, or perhaps they do not want to be seen to be connected in any way. The poet says that another avoidance tactic was to pretend to be interested in the flight of a bird overhead. The bird is described as 'fortunate'. It can fly away; it can escape any tormentors. The girls cannot. Also, the bird is graceful, unlike Tich and the poet. By looking at the bird, they can also fool themselves and others into believing that they can't hear the 'urgent conference' of the other girls deciding which of the pair is the lesser of two evils. Neither is wanted, but one must be chosen. We learn for the first time that the poet was a fat child; the others call her 'Tubby'. Nobody seems to want either and they argue among themselves, within earshot of the rejected girls.

The poet tells us that 'usually' she was chosen, not because she was wanted, but because she was not quite as bad as Tich. The word 'usually' again reinforces the idea that this humiliation was ongoing during the girls' early schooldays. Tich, being the last one left, had no choice but to 'lollop' to the back of the other team, even

though they had not selected her. She had to join their team simply by dint of being the final girl left. The onomatopoeic word 'lolloped' suggests Tich's graceless way of moving. Again, it might be humorous in another context, but it is not here. We can visualise her slow progress to the back of the group all too clearly and imagine the tortuous slowness of her gait. It does not require a lot of imagination to picture the expressions on the other girls' faces as they watched her ungainly run.

For the poet, things changed. She moved on to a different secondary school and she learned to use her academic ability to get her own revenge on the sporty types who had sneered at her in earlier days. It is interesting to note that the poet found a different way to bully, but did not learn that mockery is cruel and should be avoided. Like so many people who are picked on, she found her own way to do that to others.

At this point in the poem, there is a complete stop and a break before the last line, which stands alone. This adds dramatic effect and makes us concentrate on what is about to be said. What follows is a simple statement. 'Tich died when she was twelve.' There is no comment on this, no judgement, but we are struck by the fact that although the poet found her own way to cope, Tich never did. Her short life ended without her ever managing to be respected or liked by the other girls. The simplicity of the final line adds to the sadness. Just as Tich could not avoid her fate, we cannot avoid the tragedy of this ending. There is no attempt to soften the blow or to make sense of what happened. The fact that the last line stands alone symbolises Tich's standing alone, unwanted and unselected to the end of her brief, lonely life.

Themes

• Alienation

Neither Tich nor Tubby fits in and they are isolated from their classmates as a result of their physical shortcomings. Though they are both made miserable by the situation, they are not united in their sadness. They are even alienated from one another.

• Childhood/schooldays/difficulties of being young

Tich and Tubby's experience is one which is, unfortunately, shared by many schoolchildren. The other girls are cruel, albeit unwittingly. They want the best team members, but they don't consider the hurt caused by their behaviour.

This poem could be used to answer a question on:
• A poem I would recommend
• Youth
• A poem which deals with an important issue
• A person

But You Didn't

Remember the time you lent me your car and I dented it?
I thought you'd kill me ...
But you didn't.

Remember the time I forgot to tell you the dance was formal
and you came in jeans?
I thought you'd hate me ...
But you didn't

Remember the times I'd flirt with other boys
just to make you jealous, and you were?
I thought you'd drop me ...
But you didn't.

There were plenty of things you did to put up with me,
to keep me happy, to love me and there are so many things
I wanted to tell you when you returned from Vietnam ...
But you didn't.

Merrill Glass

Analysis

The poem opens on a conversational note. The poet addresses the subject of the poem directly, which adds a sense of intimacy and makes us, the reader, feel as if we are listening in to a private chat between two lovers.

The first three stanzas begin with questions in which the poet asks her boyfriend if he remembers certain ordinary events in their lives and in their relationship. Through the use of these questions, Merrill Glass builds up a portrait of the unknown, unseen boy. He is portrayed as being tolerant, loyal and loving. He put up with his girlfriend when she crashed his car and forgot to tell him that the dress code for a dance was formal, and he even loved her when she flirted with other boys to make him jealous. Nothing she did was truly terrible; all of it was relatively normal behaviour and indicative of the high spirits and naivety of youth. Still, much of it would have tried the patience of a less tolerant boyfriend and we feel that the narrator in this poem was lucky to have someone who stayed with her and loved her despite her youthful indiscretions.

On closer reading of these first three stanzas, we can see words which hint at a darker side to the poem: 'kill' and 'hate'. It is only when we read the last stanza that the significance of these words is made clear. There are a number of other features of these first stanzas which also make sense to us when we learn that the young man didn't return from Vietnam, such as the use of the past tense and the ellipses (…) at the end of the sentences. Ellipses are used to indicate an omission: that something is missing or has been left out. On one level, we could interpret them to mean that the young man is missing, which of course he is, but on another level we could deduce that the poet herself left something out, as is also the case. She tells us that:

there are so many things
I wanted to tell you when you returned from Vietnam …

Note the use of the present tense here in the word 'are'. The things remain unsaid because the poet's boyfriend was killed in the war and she never got the chance to tell him how much she loved him, presumably.

The ellipses also indicate melancholy longing and tell us that the poet is filled with regret for the things she never got to say to her lover. Her questions remain unanswered and the ellipses show that the sentences trail off into silence as the young man will never be able to respond to her again or discuss their shared history.

There is a strong contrast in this poem between the ordinary, everyday concerns of teens – driving, partying, flirting – and the fact that this particular young man died fighting in a war overseas. By discussing the mundane matters, Merrill Glass focuses our attention on the sort of things the boy should have been doing and also makes us realise how shockingly and abruptly he and his girlfriend were drawn into the adult world. The girl's previous concerns now seem trivial, yet we feel that it would be more appropriate for her world to revolve around cars, clothes and flirting rather than her regret and sadness at the violent, untimely death of her boyfriend.

The language in this poem is simple and straightforward and reflects the narrator's youth. We would not expect a teenager to use overly complex language or imagery and the chatty, conversational tone is what we would expect of a young girl chatting casually but affectionately with her boyfriend. The simplicity of the language also adds to the starkness of the message in the final lines. The repetition of 'But you didn't' at the end of the first three stanzas lulls us into a false sense of security. Each time it is said, it is connected to a happy ending when the young man turned the narrator's expectations on their head by not being angry whenever she did something wrong. The final time 'But you didn't' is used, therefore, is all the more shocking because the same line which had been used to highlight the boy's kindness, tolerance and  love is now used to tell us that he is dead. Like the narrator, our expectations have been shattered, but there is no happiness here. In the first three stanzas the narrator tells us of times she acted badly but was forgiven by her boyfriend; in the last stanza her only desire was to behave lovingly towards him, but she never got the chance. There is no complex imagery in this poem, nor is there the need for any.

Themes

- Regret

The poet is filled with sadness and regret because of all the things she never got a chance to tell her boyfriend. It makes us think about the fact that we never know what the future will hold and encourages us to seize the day, because tragedies happen and we may not get a chance to tell someone how much we love them.

- The effect of war

Unlike some other war poems you may have studied, such as 'Base Details' and 'Dulce et Decorum est', 'But You Didn't' concentrates on the pain felt by those left behind when a soldier is killed overseas.

This poem could be used to answer a question on:

- Love
- Death
- A poem I would recommend
- Wishes or thoughts
- A poem which deals with an important issue

Dulce et Decorum est

Bent double, like old beggars under sacks,
Knock-kneed, coughing like hags, we cursed through sludge,
Till on the haunting flares we turned our backs
And towards our distant rest began to trudge.
Men marched asleep. Many had lost their boots
But limped on, blood-shod. All went lame; all blind;
Drunk with fatigue; deaf even to the hoots
Of tired, outstripped Five-Nines that dropped behind.

Gas! GAS! Quick, boys! – An ecstasy of fumbling,
Fitting the clumsy helmets just in time;
But someone still was yelling out and stumbling
And flound'ring like a man in fire or lime ...
Dim, through the misty panes and thick green light
As under a green sea, I saw him drowning.

In all my dreams, before my helpless sight,
He plunges at me, guttering, choking, drowning.

If in some smothering dreams you too could pace
Behind the wagon that we flung him in,
And watch the white eyes writhing in his face,
His hanging face, like a devil's sick of sin;
If you could hear, at every jolt, the blood
Come gargling from the froth-corrupted lungs,
Obscene as cancer, bitter as the cud
Of vile, incurable sores on innocent tongues,
My friend, you would not tell with such high zest
To children ardent for some desperate glory,
The old Lie: Dulce et decorum est
Pro patria mori.

Wilfred Owen

Glossary

The words 'Dulce et Decorum est' are from a Latin ode written by the poet Horace around two thousand years ago. The poem ends with the full saying: 'Dulce et decorum est pro patria mori.' This means: 'It is sweet and right to die for your country.'

Flares – rockets which were sent up to burn brightly and light up any soldiers or other targets.

Distant rest – the exhausted soldiers were heading for a camp away from the front line where they would be allowed to rest for a few days.

Hoots – the noise made by shells flying overhead.

Outstripped – the men have managed to march beyond the reach of the shells which are now falling behind them.

Five-Nines – explosive shells.

Gas – poison gas which destroys the lungs within seconds.

Helmets – gas masks.

Flound'ring – floundering. Stumbling and struggling to stay upright. This word is often used to describe somebody who is struggling to stay afloat in the water, so it ties in with the idea of the soldier drowning in the poison gas.

Lime – a chalky substance which burns flesh.

Panes – the glass part of the gas masks.

Guttering – gurgling and choking. Guttering is also used to refer to a dying candle flame as it flickers. Owen probably meant to evoke both images in his use of this word.

Cud – regurgitated grass chewed by cows. The green froth bubbling from the dying man's lips reminded Owen of the cud.

Zest – enthusiasm.

Ardent – very keen.

Background

Wilfred Owen wrote this poem as a response to the pro-war poetry that was popular before and during the First World War. He wanted people to read about the realities of war and to realise that it was not a noble and exciting game full of opportunities for honour and glory.

Wilfred Owen was killed in action just one week before the First World War ended. He was twenty-five years old.

Analysis

Stanza One

In the first stanza, Owen sets the scene. The soldiers are trudging wearily back to camp where they may get a brief rest from the horrors of the front line. The soldiers, although they are young, are 'Bent double, like old beggars under sacks,/Knock-kneed, coughing like hags'. This image is in sharp contrast to what many people at the time would have associated with fighting men. There is no glamour or glory in Owen's description: some soldiers are barefoot, all are exhausted and lame as they stumble towards their 'distant rest'. Behind them, shells fall, but the men are deaf to the sound, so focused are they on getting to the camp.

The broad vowel sounds and the alliteration ensure that the pace of this first stanza is slow, reflecting the pace of the weary men who are 'Drunk with fatigue'.

Stanza Two

In the first stanza, Owen tells us that 'Men marched asleep'. In the second stanza they are awoken, but it is to a living nightmare. The soldiers are attacked with poison gas and they suddenly spring into action. The capital letters and the exclamation marks add to the sense of urgency: 'Gas! GAS!' The use of internal rhyme in this stanza – 'fumbling', 'clumsy' and 'stumbling' – focuses our attention on the men's awkward movements. In their desperate haste to put on the gas masks, the men are clumsy. In this 'ecstasy of fumbling' one soldier does not get his mask on in time. Helplessly, Owen watches as the man stumbles and chokes on the poison gas. Owen is watching through the glass eyepiece of his own gas mask and it appears to him as if the other man is drowning 'under a green sea'. This simile, in which Owen compares the clouds of green gas to a green sea, is a powerful one. It adds a sense of unreality to the scene, almost as if Owen momentarily cannot take in the reality of what he is seeing. A man is dying in front of his eyes and he can do nothing but watch.

Stanza Three

This stanza is only two lines long but it is no less powerful for that. The dreamlike, unreal quality of the previous stanza is continued here when Owen tells us that his dreams are haunted by the image of the dying man he could not save.

Stanza Four

The imagery in this stanza is chilling and horrific. The dying man is 'flung' into a wagon as he can no longer walk. The word 'flung' shows how cheap life has become and how there is no dignity afforded to the dying. This is understandable, of course, as the soldiers can do next to nothing to help their comrade. He is just another victim of the senseless waste of life that marked the First World War. There is little time for compassion.

As Owen paces behind the wagon, he sees the soldier's death throes. The man is writhing in agony, and every jolt of the wagon brings blood bubbling up from his ruined lungs.

Owen addresses the reader directly in this stanza, saying that if those who read his words could see the appalling reality of war, they would not be so quick to tell children 'the old Lie' that dying for your country is a sweet and noble end. There is nothing sweet or right about a man choking slowly to death in the back of a wagon.

Themes

- The horror and futility of war

This poem could be used to answer a question on:
- War
- A poem I would recommend
- Interesting imagery

Mid-Term Break

I sat all morning in the college sick bay
Counting bells knelling classes to a close.
At two o'clock our neighbours drove me home.

In the porch I met my father crying –
He had always taken funerals in his stride –
And Big Jim Evans saying it was a hard blow.

The baby cooed and laughed and rocked the pram
When I came in, and I was embarrassed
By old men standing up to shake my hand

And tell me they were 'sorry for my trouble,'
Whispers informed strangers I was the eldest,
Away at school, as my mother held my hand

In hers and coughed out angry tearless sighs.
At ten o'clock the ambulance arrived
With the corpse, stanched and bandaged by the nurses.

Next morning I went up into the room. Snowdrops
And candles soothed the bedside; I saw him
For the first time in six weeks. Paler now,

Wearing a poppy bruise on his left temple,
He lay in the four foot box as in his cot.
No gaudy scars, the bumper knocked him clear.

A four foot box, a foot for every year.

Seamus Heaney

Glossary

Sick bay – a place in schools (usually in boarding schools) where those students who are suffering from minor ailments can be treated.

Knelling – this describes the slow, solemn ringing of a bell, usually for funerals.

Stanched – any bleeding has been stopped.

Background

This poem is about a real event in Heaney's childhood. When he was away at boarding school in Derry, his younger brother Christopher was killed in a road accident.

Analysis

Stanza One

The poem opens with the image of the boy sitting in the school sickbay, waiting to be brought home by his neighbours. At this stage we do not know why he is being taken out of school, and on first reading the poem we may be misled by the title and the opening lines. After all, mid-term break is something most students look forward to, a welcome break from classes and schoolwork. However, the sombre tone of this stanza is our first indication that the subject of the poem may be more serious than we first supposed. We may also wonder why the boy's neighbours, and not his parents, are bringing him home.

Young Heaney has nothing to do but sit and wait, and note the passing of time as bells ring 'classes to a close'. The school bells are described as 'knelling', a word more usually associated with church bells ringing at a funeral. We can easily imagine how difficult it must have been for the boy to wait alone, and the fact

that the passing of time is mentioned, as well as the exact time –
two o'clock – that he was taken home shows how interminably long
the wait must have seemed.

Stanzas Two to Five

We realise immediately that something dreadful has happened.
The boy meets his father crying in the porch, he who had 'always
taken funerals in his stride'. In the pram, Heaney's baby sister
laughs and coos, unaware of the tragedy that has befallen the
family. This brief description of carefree happiness contrasts
starkly with the terrible sadness in the rest of the poem.

The poet is still only a boy himself and he is embarrassed to be
treated like a man by the neighbours who condole with him and
whisper to strangers that he is 'the eldest/Away at school'. This
tragedy marks a transition from child to adult for the boy. His
mother is too shocked to cry and instead coughs out 'angry
tearless sighs' as she holds his hand for support. The parents'
vulnerability in their time of grief means that young Heaney must
grow up quickly and assume a more adult role in the family.

The ambulance arrives with 'the corpse'. If we are reading the
poem for the first time, we still do not know who has died.

Stanzas Six and Seven

Next morning, the poet goes up to the room where the
corpse of his little brother is laid out. The images of the
'Snowdrops/and candles' around the bedside, and the
use of the word 'soothe' create a calm, peaceful mood.
The bruise on the little boy's temple is compared to
a flower, 'a poppy bruise', and it contrasts with the
white of the snowdrops.

In heartbreakingly simple words, Heaney
describes his dead brother lying in his
coffin 'as if in a cot'. We are reminded of the
contrast between the small, still body in the

coffin and his baby sister who 'rocked the pram'.

In the last line, we discover the age of the dead boy. He was only four when he was knocked down and killed. The last two lines are the only lines of the poem in which we find full rhyme. This brings a sense of closure to the poem, reinforcing the end of the small boy's life.

Themes

- Death, particularly sudden or tragic death
- Growing up

This poem could be used to answer a question on:
- A poem which deals with an important issue
- A poem I would recommend
- Death

QUESTION 2, SECTION 2, PAPER 2, JUNIOR CERT HL, 2010

Imagine you have to recommend one poem that you have studied for a new publication entitled, A Book of Favourite Poems for Young People of the 21st Century.

Name the poem you would choose and explain why this particular poem would be suitable for inclusion in this collection.

In your answer you may wish to consider some of the following: the poem's theme, the way the poet uses language, the imagery, tone and/or mood, the structure of the poem, etc. (30 marks)

This question helps you to plan your answer by suggesting several things you may wish to consider. Of course, you are not limited to these topics, but they should feature in your answer.

In this answer, five different points about the poem will be discussed. Between four and six points is appropriate for a thirty-mark question. Each point will be given a separate paragraph. Although there is no set length for a thirty-mark question, you should be aiming to fill around two pages of your answer book.

You could, of course, discuss this poem stanza by stanza. This approach, in which you may decide to deal with various aspects of the poem in the same paragraph, would be equally valid. Sample Answer 2 on page 228 shows how this can be done.

The points will be:

1. Theme
2. Characterisation
3. Language
4. Imagery
5. Tone

EXAM **FOCUS**   *Don't waste time writing a detailed, neat plan. Use individual words rather than sentences.*

You will notice that many sentences in this answer are taken directly from the notes on the poem. While it is not a good idea for you to take credit for the work of others, this does show you that if you prepare and write notes on your chosen poems in advance, you will be well able to answer any question in the examination.

Sample Answer 1

Name the poet and the poem in the opening lines of the answer

Point 1: theme. Relate it back to the question by mentioning that it is relevant to young people

If I had to recommend one poem for inclusion in a publication entitled A Book of Favourite Poems for Young People of the 21st Century, *I would choose Wendy Cope's 'Tich Miller'.*

This poem deals with the cruelty of schoolchildren and the effect that being isolated and unwanted can have on the victims of bullying. Although this sad theme may not seem to make the poem a likely candidate for inclusion in a book of favourite poems, I think it is well-liked because people can relate to it. It makes us think. Tich and Tubby's experience is one which is, unfortunately, shared by many young people. Neither girl fits in and they are alienated from their classmates as a result of their physical shortcomings. Tich has 'one foot three sizes larger than the other', while the unkind nickname 'Tubby' tells its own story.

As well as having a theme which is relevant to almost anyone who is still at school, this poem draws a very realistic and sympathetic portrait of Tich. The language used to describe Tich is economical and matter-of-fact, but it is no less powerful for that. In the first three lines the poet paints an accurate and heart-breaking picture of the girl in glasses with ugly 'elastoplast-pink frames'. The use of Tich's name in the opening words of the poem makes us feel connected with a real girl who feels the hurt of being unwanted.

Point 2: characterisation. Linking paragraphs in an essay-style answer increases your chance of getting high marks by showing the examiner that your work is planned and organised

It is this simplicity of language which makes 'Tich Miller' ideally suited for a book of poetry for young people. It is easily understood and accessible to all. The use of dialogue in the fourth stanza, when the other girls are urgently debating the merits of one unwanted team member over another, adds immediacy and drama to the poem: ' "Have Tubby!" "No, no, have Tich!" '

Point 3: language, and the way it makes this poem accessible to young people

The simplicity of the language does not detract from the powerful imagery. The description of Tich and Tubby 'affecting interest in the flight/of some fortunate bird' is particularly moving. It is easy to visualise the two girls, trapped and powerless, watching and envying the effortless grace of the bird which can escape any tormentors. The girls cannot. They are trapped behind the 'wire-mesh fence'. Tich and Tubby are caged, while the bird flies free.

Point 4: Imagery. The bird's flight shows us how trapped the girls are by comparison

The matter-of-fact nature of the language does not detract from the poignant, heart-rending tone of the poem. Although Wendy Cope relates the happenings in an unemotional way, the emotional impact of the words cannot be ignored. She describes Tich as having 'lolloped, unselected,/to the back of the other team'. The mood of the poem is brilliantly captured in these two lines.

Point 5: tone. Use words which might describe a person's mood when describing tone

Tich is clumsy and unwanted. Her rejection is obvious and embarrassing. There is a bitterness, too, in the way Tubby says that she is chosen first only because she is 'the lesser dud'.

The final point comments on the way the poem ends and the effect this has on the reader

At this point in the poem, there is a complete stop and a break before the last line, which stands alone. This adds dramatic effect and makes us concentrate on what is about to be said. What follows is a simple statement. 'Tich died when she was twelve.' There is no comment on this, no judgement, but we are struck by the fact that, while the poet found her own way to cope, Tich never did. The simplicity of the final line adds to the sadness. There is no attempt to soften the blow or to make sense of what happened. The fact that the last line stands alone symbolises Tich's standing alone, unwanted and unselected to the end of her brief, lonely life.

Brief conclusion refers back to the wording of the question

This is a poem which, although it may be challenging and upsetting, makes the reader think. I feel sure that it would be as memorable for all young people who may read it in a collection as it has been for me.

Question

Choose two poems which deal with a similar theme. Name the poems, poet(s) and theme dealt with and discuss how each poem deals with the theme. (30 marks)

Sample Answer 2

Poets and poems clearly named. Wording of question reflected in underlined section

The poems which I have chosen are Seamus Heaney's 'Mid-Term Break' and Merrill Glass's 'But You Didn't'. Both poems deal with the theme of death but each poet approaches the issue differently. Seamus Heaney recalls how he felt when, as a child himself, he was called home from school after the tragic death of his little brother, and Merrill Glass remembers a boyfriend who was killed in the Vietnam war.

In both poems, it is only at the end that we truly realise the enormity of the poet's loss and the fact that the person who died was young and should have lived for many more years. 'But You Didn't' offers no hints of the seriousness of its theme at the beginning of the poem, while we do suspect that something has happened in 'Mid-Term Break' when Heaney refers to the bells in school 'knelling classes to a close'. The use of the word 'knelling' suggests a funeral.

In contrast to the early introduction of the solemn mood in 'Mid-Term Break', Glass's 'But You Didn't' opens in a chatty, conversational tone, which continues right up to the last stanza. Unlike Heaney, Glass addresses the subject of the poem directly, asking if he remembers a series of trivial events in their relationship. She begins all of these anecdotes in the same way, 'Remember the time ...?' This use of questions throughout the poem gives the work a sense of intimacy and makes us feel that we are listening in to a private conversation between the two lovers. Like Heaney's reference to the 'knelling' bells, however, there is a hint of the poem's theme in the first stanza: 'I thought you'd kill me.'

Although 'Mid-Term Break' also deals with the sudden, shocking, untimely death of a young person, Heaney holds back from sharing his thoughts with us in the same way Glass does. Instead, he focuses on the reactions of those around him. He talks of his father crying, his father who had 'always taken funerals in his stride'. He describes his mother's 'angry tearless sighs' as she holds his hand and he tells us of the neighbours who offer him their condolences and whisper that he is 'the eldest,/Away at school'. The formality and ritual associated with Heaney's brother's death contrasts with the chatty, informal way in which Glass addresses the issue.

However, both poems come together in their shocking, stark endings. Few people could fail to be moved when Heaney describes his baby brother lying in his coffin, 'A four foot box, a foot for every year.' Although we had known that there had been a

Comparing and contrasting the way in which the two poets introduce the theme of death

Quotes are used and they are worked into the fabric of the sentences whenever possible. Also, each quotation is explained in the context of the answer. It is not simply left hanging there

Quotes, when they are used, are not lengthy, but they are relevant

death in the family, not until the very end of the poem do we realise that this poem is about the death of a very small boy. Similarly, Glass startles us with her final line about the boy she intended to talk to at length when he came home from Vietnam, 'But you didn't.' Neither poem deliberately wrings our emotions, but rather, through the use of simple, clear language, they outline the facts for us. Death is shocking and it is hard to understand the reason behind it. Those who are left behind are forever changed by the experience and carry it with them in their memories always.

I enjoyed both 'Mid-Term Break' and 'But You Didn't' and I found them among the most memorable poems on my course.

Paragraphs are linked and follow a plan. Each one deals with a different aspect of the poems and each looks at the way both poems deal with the theme (reflecting the question)

Conclusion refers back to wording of question and links poems again. Note personal response

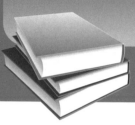

UNSEEN FICTION

The Unseen Fiction section of Paper 2 is worth **30 marks**.

You should spend about **25 minutes** on this section.

Total: **30**

It is important to realise that this section, which can seem the easiest, requires the same level of attention as the drama and poetry questions. It is not simply a comprehension; that is tested in Paper 1. Here, you are asked questions on plot, characters, style, setting, etc. In other words, many of the same things that come up in the drama and poetry sections. Use literary terms in your answers and support everything you say by referring closely to the text.

You might have seen this extract before: perhaps it is from a short story or novel you have read. If so, remember to stick to the text in front of you when answering the questions; don't use any other knowledge than can be gained from reading the extract.

EXAM **FOCUS**   *Don't forget to quote. Keep the quotes short and integrate them into the sentence.*

TYPICAL QUESTIONS AND HOW TO APPROACH THEM

Plot

The plot is the series of events that ties the story together and gives it meaning.

There are several different ways in which the plot may be arranged; the author may simply place the events in chronological order (the order in which they happened) or he or she may use techniques such as flashbacks.

A question on plot may ask you to predict an ending. See what clues you are given in the extract.

Character

As discussed in the Studied Drama chapter, look at the characters closely. How are they described? Does what they say or do tell us anything about them? Does what others say about them give us any insights? The most common questions are those on character. Look for the aspects of character mentioned in Chapter 7 (page 158) and also see if there are any contradictions in the character's personality. Are they hypocritical? Do they say one thing but do another? If the character is a bully, for example, are they morally weak but physically strong? How do the characters react to the events that occur in the extract? How do other characters react to the character you are examining? Descriptions of their body language can tell us a lot, as can the way the characters talk to one another.

It is important to be able to identify some common characteristics and to use the correct words when describing them. The list below may help:

Boastful, bossy, brave, bullying, belligerent, decent, deceitful, mannerly, unpleasant, cowardly, passionate, cruel, polite, kind, ruthless, stubborn, powerful, protective, humble, horrible, dominant, entertaining, pathetic, honest, honourable, respectful, boring, naïve, nasty, inspirational, insensitive, sensitive, villainous, fiendish, glamorous, needy, nervous, relaxed, strong, weak.

Obviously, you will be able to think of more descriptions to add to this list.

Use synonyms (words which have the same meaning) rather than repeating the same words throughout your answer. For example, synonyms of bossy include controlling, domineering, overbearing, pushy and high-handed.

Relationships

You may be asked to comment on the relationships between central characters in your chosen text.

Setting

Look at when and where the story takes place. This can give you a context to the issues the characters may be facing. The setting can also help to create a certain atmosphere; think of horror films you have seen, for example.

Style

Look at all the language used and analyse it carefully. For more details on how to approach a style question, refer back to the Reading and Poetry chapters of this book.

QUESTION 1, **SECTION 3, PAPER 2, JUNIOR CERT HL, 2011**

Read the extract below and then answer the questions which follow.

The following edited extract is adapted from the award-winning novel, *Mister Pip*, by Lloyd Jones.

Matilda is a young girl who lives in Bougainville, a tropical island that has been ravaged by civil war. The tiny local school has been closed for a number of months due to the fighting. In this extract Mr Watts, also known as Pop Eye, a self-appointed teacher, has decided to reopen the school.

'Get up Matilda,' my mum yelled one morning. 'You've got school today.' She must have enjoyed that moment. I could tell it cheered her up just to say it. As if we had slipped back into a comfortable old routine. I happened to know it was a Wednesday. My mum wouldn't have known that. I kept a pencil under my mat. And a calendar of days on the corner post. Eighty-six days had passed since my last day at school.

My mum swept her broom near my head. She shouted at a rooster that had flown in the door. 'But we have no teachers,' I said. And with a glimmer of a smile, my mum said, 'You do now. Pop Eye is going to teach you kids.'

Pop Eye was waiting for us inside. It was almost dark, though light enough to make out the tall thin white man in his linen suit. He stood at the front of the class, his eyes glancing away from our inspection. His hair was long, nearly touching his shoulders. When it was short we hadn't noticed the flecks of red and grey. His beard spilled down onto his chest.

He looked at our faces, taking each of us in, though careful not to linger. Just noting who had turned up. I had never heard him speak. As far as I knew, no one in that class had. I don't know what I was expecting, except when he spoke his voice was surprisingly small. He spoke as if he was addressing each one of us personally.

'I want this to be a place of light,' he said. 'No matter what happens.'

'We must clear the space and make it ready for learning,' he said. 'Make it new again.' We swept out the classroom. We were enjoying our first day back at school. Mr Watts kept an eye on us. He allowed high spirits. But when he spoke we shut up.

Now we returned to our desks to wait for him to dismiss us and send us home. He spoke in that same quiet voice that had come as as such a surprise at the start of the day.

'I want you to understand something. I am no teacher, but I will do my best. That's my promise to you children. I believe, with your parents' help, we can make a difference to our lives.'

He stopped there like he'd just had a new thought, and he must have, because next he asked us to get up from our desks and to form a circle. He told us to hold hands or link arms, whatever we saw fit. There was no prayer. There was no sermon. Instead, Mr Watts thanked us all for turning up. 'I wasn't sure you would,' he said. 'I will be honest with you. I have no wisdom, none at all. The truest thing I can tell you is that whatever we have between us is all we've got. Oh, and of course, Mr Dickens.'

[The next day] we sat at our desks and waited for Mr Watts to introduce Mr Dickens. He wasn't there when we arrived. There was just Mr Watts, as we had found him the day before, standing tall at the front of the class, lost in a dream. While we waited for Mr Watts to wake from his dream I counted three lime-green geckos. A flower-pecker bird flew in the open window and out again. As the bird flew out the window, Mr Watts began to read to us.

I had never been read to in English before. Nor had the others. We didn't have books in our homes, and before the blockade our only books had come from Moresby, and those were written in pidgin*. When Mr Watts read to us we fell quiet. It was a new sound in the world. He read slowly so we heard the shape of each word.

'My father's family name being Pirrip, and my Christian name Philip, my infant tongue could make of both names nothing longer or more explicit than Pip. So I called myself Pip, and came to be called Pip.'

There had been no warning from Mr Watts. He just began to read. My desk was in the second row from the back. Gilbert Masoi sat in front, and I couldn't see past his fat shoulders and big woolly head.

So when I heard Mr Watts speak I thought he was talking about himself. That he was Pip. It was only as he began to walk between our desks that I saw the book in his hand.

He kept reading and we kept listening. It was some time before he stopped, but when he looked up we sat stunned by the silence. The flow of words had ended. Slowly we stirred back into our bodies and our lives. Mr Watts closed the book and held the paperback up in one hand like a church minister. 'That was chapter one of *Great Expectations*, which, incidentally, is the greatest novel by the greatest English writer of the nineteenth century, Charles Dickens.'

pidgin – a language made up of elements of two or more languages

*Answer **two** of the following questions. Each question is worth 15 marks.*

1. Do you think Mr Watts will be a good teacher? Base your answer on what you have read in the above extract.

2. Based on what you have read in this extract, describe Bougainville and explain why you would or would not like to live there.

3. Imagine that Mr Watts (and not Matilda) is the narrator of this passage. Write an account of his first day's teaching as seen through his eyes.

Sample Answer 1

1. Do you think Mr Watts will be a good teacher? Base your answer on what you have read in the above extract. (15)

When you are planning your answer, try to work from the start of the extract through to the end. This will ensure that your answer is well structured.

Even though this is not a piece of drama or poetry, you will still be expected to quote or to refer closely to the text to support the points you make.

This question asks for a personal response, but every point must be based on the extract

Keep referring back to the question and saying why you believe the points you raise mean that Mr Watts will be a good teacher

I think that Mr Watts will make a good teacher because he is clearly committed to the job and wants to do his best for his pupils. He has volunteered to take the post, even though he admits that he is unqualified and has 'no wisdom, none at all'. That he should want to teach despite having to learn as he goes along is, I feel, a good sign. I believe that his dream of making the school 'a place of light' is a very positive one and that such enthusiasm and dedication to education will pay off in the end.

Another reason that I would be hopeful about Mr Watts' chances of success is that he clearly has an instant rapport* with the children. He knows enough to allow them to indulge in 'high spirits' when they are cleaning the room but they fall silent the moment he begins to speak. He seems to have an instinctive knowledge of how to hold his pupils' attention. The fact that he is honest with them, 'I am no teacher', but at the same time promises to do his best is something that is likely to appeal to the class. He uses the word 'we' and 'our' when talking about his plans, which shows that he wants to work with the children to 'make a difference' to their lives.

Don't simply list his good points and leave it at that. Say what such attributes would be likely to mean to the pupils

While Mr Watts is dedicated, honest and commands the pupils' respect, that would not be enough to hold the children's attention for long if he did not have any interesting material to teach. Fortunately, he does. I think that his choice of Dickens' Great Expectations is a good one because Mr Watts loves it himself and calls it 'the greatest novel by the greatest English writer of the nineteenth century'. His passion for the book seems infectious and the children listen to it in rapt silence. I believe that any teacher who can make pupils lose themselves in literature to the extent that Mr Watts does is bound to be a success at his job.

Vary your vocabulary: say 'pupils', 'students', 'children' and 'class' rather than just using one word throughout

*rapport – relationship of mutual trust and liking

Sample Answer 2

2. Based on what you have read in this extract, describe Bougainville and explain why you would or would not like to live there. (15)

Note that you are asked to do two things in this question. First, you must **describe Bougainville**, and second, you must say **whether or not it would appeal to you as a place to live**.

Bougainville, as it is described in this extract, is an island which has suffered badly as a result of civil war. The infrastructure seems almost non-existent, whether because of the war or because the island is under-developed is not clear. Matilda's house sounds very basic. She sleeps on a mat, chickens fly in and out of the house, and her mother does not even have any means of telling the date. This probably means that there are no communications systems on the island. There doesn't seem to be any electricity as Matilda says that when she went into school 'it was almost dark, though light enough to make out the tall thin white man'.

The impression of Bougainville as being a poor place is supported by the lack of education available to the children. There are no professional teachers in the school and instead the pupils and parents must rely on a volunteer who is the first to admit that he is 'no teacher' and has 'no wisdom, none at all'.

However, despite the lack of what most of us would view as necessities, Bougainville does have a certain appeal and I think it is somewhere I would like to live. First, the lack of teachers is not necessarily something that makes the place unattractive to me! Although if I am honest, I would eventually tire of all that free time and would be pleased that someone in the local community was willing to take on the job of schoolmaster. Mr Watts' volunteering to do so and the obvious support he has from parents and students alike shows that Bougainville has a strong, close community.

There are other attractions besides the people. Bougainville is

When you say something about Bougainville, make sure that you give a reason for your opinion, using reference to the extract

a tropical island and I found the descriptions of the exotic wildlife enchanting. I would love to live in a place where, from my desk, I could count 'lime-green geckos' and watch the wonderfully named 'flower-pecker bird'. Perhaps I have a romantic idea of life on a tropical island, but it does sound like a place I would happily spend my life.

Sample Answer 3

3. Imagine that Mr Watts (and not Matilda) is the narrator of this passage. Write an account of his first day's teaching as seen through his eyes. (15)

This account would most likely be written in the form of a diary entry. A diary entry is simply a record of the writer's own thoughts and feelings about a particular event. Imagine you are Mr Watts and are describing this day to a close friend or family member. What would you say?

Make sure you base your ideas on the passage. There are lots of hints in there to help you.

It is appropriate in a piece like this to give the person's reflections on the events that have taken place

It is evening and I am sitting on the porch, looking at the sun setting over the ocean. Hard to believe, viewing this idyllic scene, that only a few miles away and a few weeks ago men fought and died for this place. Perhaps that is something that a teacher should be able to discuss with students. I will not. I do not feel qualified.

Speaking of not being qualified, I wonder if it was wise to admit that to the children yesterday. Not that most of them didn't

All the points raised are based on the passage. Matilda says that she has never heard Mr Watts speak and that she thinks none of the other children have either

already suspect my lack of credentials, of course. But I have managed to maintain a certain amount of privacy and, dare I say it, a sense of mystery, in this place until yesterday. Perhaps I could have fooled them. I don't think I have ever spoken to those youngsters, or they to me. Until yesterday. But once I saw them all there early in the morning, so eager and willing, it seemed wrong to pretend to be anything I am not.

They are marvellous, those children. They swept the room thoroughly, even if they were slightly rowdy. It was nothing more than high spirits, really. I left them to it and I was quietly pleased to see how attentively they listened once their task was completed. Their willingness to work together and to work with me filled me with hope. I felt that it was our school and our future. I tried to tell them as much and to emphasise the fact that we could make a difference. We could change things for the better and make our world anew.

Tomorrow I will read them Dickens. They deserve it, and I believe they will at least give it a chance. With luck, they will share even a portion of my love for his work. I can think of no greater gift to give them.

The extract covers two days, but the question only asks you to mention the first day

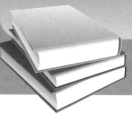

STUDIED FICTION

The Studied Fiction section of Paper 2 is worth **30 marks**.

You should spend about **25 minutes** on this section.

Refer back to the chapter on Studied Drama (page 158) to see how the five questions described there can help you to prepare for and answer your Studied Fiction question.

Although there is no length specified for this question, it is worth 30 marks and should therefore contain around six paragraphs and take up approximately two pages of your answer book.

TYPICAL QUESTIONS AND HOW TO PREPARE FOR THEM

Character

You should have reasonably detailed notes on each of the main characters. Try to organise these notes under headings, so that when you come to revise them, you will be able to scan quickly through the headings and remind yourself of the main points about each character. You might also want to consider whether your chosen characters are dynamic or static. If they are dynamic, they change and develop as the story progresses. If they are static, they remain the same throughout the story.

A good way to revise your chosen characters is to ask yourself the five questions shown below and write answers to each. Then, if you are asked an essay-style question on the characters, you will be likely to structure the answer well. Ask yourself these questions in the exam, too:

1. How is the character **introduced** and what is our first

impression of him or her?

2. Does the character have to face any **challenges** and, if so, how does he or she react to them?

3. Does the character have to deal with a major **crisis** at a turning point in the story?

4. How is the crisis **resolved** and what role does the character play in the resolution (if any)?

5. What is our **final impression** of the character and is it different from our initial impression?

Websites such as SparkNotes, BBC GCSE Bitesize and LitCharts can be a great source of notes on your chosen texts.

EXAM **FOCUS**

Relationships

You should be able to discuss the relationships between the major characters. Again, the five question rule will help you prepare for this question.

1. How is the relationship **introduced**?

2. Are there **challenges** or difficulties which threaten the relationship?

Always read the exam paper carefully before you begin

3. Is there a moment of **crisis** in the relationship?

4. How is the crisis **resolved**?

5. What state is the relationship in at the **end** of the text?

Prepare notes on a good relationship and a bad relationship in your chosen text.

EXAM **FOCUS**

Theme

You should know the theme, or the main message, of your chosen text. Although there may be many themes in the text, you should concentrate on the major ones. Racial prejudice, for example, is central to *Roll of Thunder, Hear My Cry,* while friendship and the impossibility of dreams are central to *Of Mice and Men.*

At this stage, you will be unsurprised to hear that the five question rule also applies to questions on theme.

1. How is the theme **introduced**?
2. Is the theme **developed** as the characters face **challenges** or **difficulties**?
3. Is there a moment of **crisis** when the theme is clearly shown?
4. What does the **resolution** of the crisis tell us about the theme?
5. What have we learned about the theme by the **end of the story** and what is the **final message**?

Key moments

Think of the five questions here. Most key moments can be found at one of these points in the text. Be prepared to discuss any of these key moments and their importance in terms of the overall plot. Look particularly closely at the opening and the ending of the text. Did the opening intrigue you and set the scene well, for example? Was the ending satisfactory? Were all loose ends neatly tied up or was there an open ending?

EXAM **FOCUS**   *Key quotes are a great help in your answer on Studied Fiction. Keep them short and relevant.*

Mood or atmosphere

You may be asked to discuss a section of the text which is happy, sad, tense, light-hearted or serious, for example.

Conflict

Be prepared to discuss conflict between characters and have in mind a number of key moments when this conflict is clearly shown. It is a good idea to think in terms of plot structure when answering your questions as it can help you to stay focused.

Depending on the question, it may not be necessary to mention every aspect of the plot. Use your own judgement here.

Social setting

You may be asked to comment on the world of the text and you should be ready to say why you would or would not like to live in that world. The sorts of things you should consider are:

- The time period in which the story is set
- The place where the story is set
- The political background, if relevant. Is there a war on, for example?
- The way women and children are treated
- Is there prejudice or injustice in the world of the text?
- What are the people's religious beliefs? Do they affect their actions?
- Who holds the most power in the world of the text? Is it wealthy men, for example?

Style

Be prepared to comment on the way in which your chosen text is written.

Review

Be able to say why you would recommend this text to people of your own age. Consider each of the points given above. For example, you might want to talk about the theme(s), the characters, the relationships, and what you learned about the world of the text. That gives you five points to discuss. You could add more, of course.

QUESTION 2, SECTION 3, PAPER 2, JUNIOR CERT HL, 2011

From the short stories or novels you have studied, choose one in which the setting (time and place) is either similar to or different from the time and place in which you live.

(a) Give a detailed description of the setting of the short story or novel. (15 marks)

(b) How is the setting of the short story or novel similar to or different from the time and place in which you live? In your answer refer closely to your studied text. (15 marks)

Sample Answer 1

2(a). Give a detailed description of the setting of the short story or novel. (15)

This opening paragraph could be used for any answer on this novel

The novel I have studied is Harper Lee's To Kill A Mockingbird. *The story takes place in the fictional town of Maycomb, Alabama during the Great Depression of the 1930s. The narrator is Scout Finch, who lives with her brother Jem and her widowed father Atticus.*

Each point you make must be supported by reference to the novel

Maycomb is a 'tired old town' where there is little to do. The Depression has left the people with 'nothing to buy and no money to buy it with'. The people in the town know each other well, and they know everyone's family history. This small-town attitude shapes the characters and the plot. Certain people are viewed as being possessed of certain traits simply because of their family background. Even the rational Atticus says of the Ewell family that they have been 'the disgrace of Maycomb for three generations' and so it is pointless to expect Burris Ewell to attend school.

The Ewells are at the bottom of a complicated class hierarchy in Maycomb. Near the top are the Finches as they are quite well-off and educated. Aunt Alexandra does her best to ensure that the social order remains as it is and tells Scout not to play with Walter Cunningham because 'he is trash'. Everyone in Maycomb feeds into the system. The townspeople are seen as superior to the farmers, and white trash, like the Ewells, are at the very bottom of the pecking order, even below the Cunninghams. Mayella Ewell is lonely and isolated because the white people consider her too low-class to mix with and the black people won't have anything to do with her as she is white.

Maycomb, like any town in the American South during the 1930s, is segregated. Black people do not have the same rights as white people, nor do they attend the same schools or churches. Racism and prejudice are rife, and when Tom Robinson, a black man, is accused of raping Mayella Ewell, he is found guilty despite an almost total lack of evidence. The fact that Tom Robinson is even allowed a trial infuriates some of the white people, who would prefer to see the black man lynched by a local mob.

Maycomb may appear little more than a sleepy old town, but it is a place where poverty and prejudice hold sway and where the setting has an enormous influence on the lives of everyone in the novel.

Sample Answer 2

2(b). How is the setting of the short story or novel similar to or different from the time and place in which you live? In your answer refer closely to your studied text. (15)

Maycomb, Alabama in the 1930s is a very different place from twenty-first-century Ireland.

Certainly, there are small towns in Ireland where everybody

State your position in the opening sentence

Stick to the text as much as possible. Although you must compare the setting of the text to the world in which you live, do not bring in irrelevant factors such as lack of modern technology in 1930s Maycomb, for example

knows everybody else's business and families have connections which go back for many generations, but I do not believe this is a limiting factor in people's lives in the same way it is for the people of Maycomb. For example, Burris Ewell's family's refusal to send him to school is not something which would be so readily accepted in present-day Ireland. Atticus says that 'it's silly to force people like the Ewells into a new environment', but I disagree. By simply allowing the Ewells to continue living in ignorance and squalor, the people of Maycomb unwittingly allow a situation to develop in which the lonely, abused Mayella causes Tom Robinson's wrongful imprisonment and death.

Always try to link your points

Another aspect of the setting of the novel which is different from the world in which I live is the class system. Again, this is seen as a limiting factor in people's lives and people from a higher class are not meant to associate with people from a lower class. I have never come across someone like Aunt Alexandra: a woman who is so prejudiced that she only wants Scout and Jem to mix with 'fine folks' and is prepared to speak cruelly about young children like Walter Cunningham and Dill.

While the snobbery and class system in Maycomb might be unpleasant, it is nothing like as unpleasant as the racial prejudice shown so clearly in the shameful treatment of Tom Robinson. Racism is something which does exist in Ireland, unfortunately, but it is not written into law in the same way as it was in the southern states of the USA in the 1930s. It is not just the poorly educated people in To Kill A Mockingbird who support segregation and racial hatred. The teacher, Miss Gates, says that Hitler is evil for persecuting the Jews, but Scout has heard her saying that black people are getting above themselves and need to be taught a lesson before they come to believe they are equal to white people. I have never heard anyone speak this way and, if they were to do so, I do not believe it would be easily and readily agreed with the way it is in Maycomb.

In conclusion, I think that the setting in To Kill A Mockingbird is restrictive and unfair and does not allow people to reach their full potential unless they are lucky enough to be born the right colour and born into the right family. This, I believe, is the difference between the world of the novel and the world in which I live. Even though life in Ireland may not be perfect, everybody is entitled to be treated fairly and equally.

QUESTION 2, SECTION 3, PAPER 2, JUNIOR CERT HL, 2009

Select a novel or short story you have studied which has an interesting theme.

(a) Outline the theme of the text you have chosen. (15 marks)

(b) As the theme develops, why does it interest you? (15 marks)

Sample Answer 1

1(a). Outline the theme of the text you have chosen. (15)

The novel I have studied is Mildred D. Taylor's Roll of Thunder, Hear My Cry. *The novel is set in Mississippi during the Great Depression of the 1930s and is narrated by Cassie Logan, a nine-year-old black girl living on her family's farm. The theme which I find particularly interesting in this text is racial discrimination.*

You must always name the novel and the author in the opening sentence

The theme is introduced early in the novel when Cassie and her siblings are walking to school. They have to walk as, unlike the white children, those who attend the all-black school do not have a bus. As well as being discriminated against in this way, the black children also have a shorter school year so that they can work on the farms, and many of them do not complete their education because they must leave school and work to support their families. Even the books they use in class show how little black children's education is valued by the authorities. Books are passed down through a number of white children over time until they become so old and worn that they are not considered fit for white students.

Explain how the theme is introduced

Explain how the theme is developed

At that stage they are marked 'nigra' and passed on to the black schools.

As the novel progresses we learn that racial discrimination can have far more serious consequences than the unfair allocation of school books. A neighbour of the Logans, John Henry Berry, is set on fire by white men because they believe that he flirted with a white woman. His agonising death goes unpunished, even though everyone knows that the white Wallace family are responsible.

This is the moment of highest tension in the novel

The Logans boycott the Wallace's store as a protest against this violent act, but they in turn are threatened by the powerful white landowner, Harlan Granger, who says that all the white farmers will raise their rents on land farmed by black families if the boycott continues.

Tensions between the black and white communities run high and Cassie has her own experience with prejudice when she is humiliated by Lillian Jean Simms and her father and is forced to treat the white girl as a superior simply because of her colour. Although Cassie gets her revenge on the other girl, this is only a tiny victory.

The Wallace and Simms families cause great trouble for their black neighbours. The Wallaces attack Cassie's father, leaving him injured and unable to farm his land. The Simms brothers lead T.J., a foolish and lonely black boy, astray and make him the fall guy for their murder of a white shopkeeper.

All of this racial discrimination culminates in white vigilantes going to T.J.'s house with the intention of lynching him. In order to prevent this racially motivated murder, Cassie's father sets fire to his fields, causing all the locals, black and white, to rush to stop the spread of the fire. The two communities are brought together briefly but T.J. still faces trial for murder. The best Cassie's father could do was to spare him from the lynch mob. The novel ends on a sombre note and there is no sense that racial discrimination will cease, or even lessen.

Sample Answer 2

1(b). As the theme develops, why does it interest you? (15)

The development of the theme interested me at every stage of the novel. The introduction of the theme is through a series of relatively minor events which affect Cassie and her friends but have little impact on the rest of the characters. As Cassie is a nine-year-old girl, it seems fitting that she should only focus on those things which directly affect her. Through incidents such as the white children's bus covering the black children with dust and mud or Little Man refusing to accept a tattered old school book, we are gradually led into a world where racial prejudice and discrimination are rife.

As the story develops, the racial discrimination becomes more serious and, although Cassie's family try to protect the young girl from some of the worst horrors, such as the burning of John Henry Berry by the night men, it is impossible to keep such stories from her. Thus we see that the evil that racial discrimination brings with it taints Cassie's childhood and drags her and the other children into the darker side of the adult world long before their time.

I was fascinated and horrified by the way in which so many adults in the novel seem to accept racial injustice and the intimidation of black people as the norm. The white community in general supports the Wallaces, even though they know that they are violent criminals. Even Big Ma tells Cassie to apologise to Lillian Jean Simms in Strawberry, despite the fact that Cassie did nothing wrong. Having read the novel, I began to understand the helplessness that some black people must have felt in the face of overwhelming prejudice. After all, even the law of the land said that segregation was right and proper.

Cassie is an ideal narrator because as she encounters incidents of racial prejudice and has to have them explained to her by her family, we, the readers, learn too. I liked Cassie's spirit and her

You must ensure that you say why you found the theme interesting

The question asks you to focus on the development of the theme, so go through the relevant events of the novel in chronological order

refusal to simply accept discrimination as a part of life. Yet, through her, I also learned how much people can suffer in their quest for justice and equality.

I think one of the most interesting and also one of the saddest aspects of the development of the theme was the way in which the reader is not led to believe that there is any quick fix for the problem of racial prejudice. Although Cassie's father saves T.J. from a lynch mob at the end of the novel, we learn that T.J. will be tried for murder and may even face the death penalty. There is no happy ending here, but I think that is appropriate. The issue of racial discrimination is still a major theme in the lives of the Logans and their neighbours, and their troubles are not yet over.

QUESTION 2, SECTION 3, PAPER 2, JUNIOR CERT HL, 2007

From a novel or short story you have read describe a character that impressed you, and explain why this character did so. (30 marks)

Note the word 'and' in this question. This is important as it means that there are two parts to this question. First you must describe the character you have chosen, and second you must say what it is about their character that impressed you.

Sample Answer

The novel I have studied is John Steinbeck's novella* Of Mice and Men and the character I have chosen to discuss is George, a migrant worker in 1930s California. He is travelling with his childhood friend, the mentally disabled Lennie. The pair are poor and powerless and have a difficult life. It is the way in which George copes with the troubles they face that impressed me most.

George is a smart, capable man who is well able to find work and who would probably have a better and easier life if he were not saddled with the burden of Lennie. George is only human, and he sometimes admits to feeling trapped in this relationship, saying to Lennie, 'I could get along so easy and nice if I didn't have you on my tail. I could live so easy and maybe have a girl.' However, for all his grumbling, George is devoted to Lennie and conscientiously takes care of him in every way he can. His sense of responsibility towards his companion means that he loyally sticks by him, even when Lennie is in serious trouble. The men were chased out of a place called Weed when Lennie assaulted a woman there, but George managed to get them both to safety before they could be caught. I admire this decency and the fact that no matter what happens, George never abandons Lennie.

One of the other aspects of George's character that makes him impressive, in my view, is the idealistic way he dreams of and works towards a better future. Life may be bleak now but he is saving and planning and intends to buy a little place of his own where he and Lennie can live together. It is touching the way George always includes Lennie in this vision of the perfect life. Although he may have moments of anger and irritation when he accuses Lennie of holding him back, he regrets such outbursts and claims that he is actually lucky to have Lennie: 'We got a future. We got somebody to talk to that gives a damn about us.'

George does his best to protect Lennie when they get a job at the ranch. We learn that he has been doing this since the death of Lennie's Aunt Clara and that he, George, did not always treat Lennie well. He admits to Slim that he once got Lennie to jump into a river just so he could show off to his friends and he regrets having abused the simple man for his own amusement. This shows that George is someone who learns a moral lesson from his mistakes and I think this makes him worthy of respect. He may be moody and gruff, but George is a good person with a strong conscience.

As the story progresses, George is put under more and more pressure to protect Lennie, particularly from the mean-tempered

You will need to discuss certain key moments in the story to support your points, but make sure that you do not simply give a summary of the plot. A couple of lines is fine. Remember, the examiners are familiar with the texts that are commonly chosen for study

Every time you mention something George does, say what that shows us about his character and why you find him impressive as a result

Curley, their boss's son. When Curley attacks Lennie, George tells Lennie to fight back and then, when Lennie crushes Curley's hand, George reassures him that it was not his fault. George does his best for Lennie, even though life at the ranch is becoming increasingly tense, especially with the added complication of Curley's wife, who acts like a magnet to Lennie. I don't think there are many people who would defend Lennie the way George does. He is a true friend.

This friendship and love is put to the ultimate test in the final chapter. Lennie has killed Curley's wife by accident and the ranch hands are hunting him down. It is obvious that they will kill him without mercy. George takes matters into his own hands and finds Lennie at the spot they had designated as a meeting place, should anything go wrong. George does all he can to console Lennie, assuring him that he didn't do anything wrong. He shoots Lennie quickly, while the other man is looking towards the imaginary farm they will have together. George's chance of happiness dies with Lennie. The dream is over. Although it was a tragic and violent end for Lennie, I think that George was right to spare his friend a cruel death at the hands of Curley's lynch mob.

Of Mice and Men is not an easy or an uplifting book, but the one positive thing I found in it was George's unwavering love and loyalty. He is a truly impressive character.

*novella – a short novel

The author and publisher wish to thank the following for permission to reproduce their works in this book.

U2 by U2 reprinted by permission of HarperCollins Publishers Ltd, © 2006 U2 Limited; *The Irish Times* for permission to reproduce *Shhhhhh!* by Hugh Linehan; 'The Same Old Moon' by Geraldine Aron, reproduced by permission of The Agency London Ltd, © Geraldine Aron, all rights reserved; 'Cinders' by Roger McGough, from *Defying Gravity,* © Roger McGough 1992, reproduced by permission of United Agents on behalf of Roger McGough; 'Cinders' from *Defying Gravity* by Roger McGough, © Roger McGough 1992, Viking, reprinted by permission of Peters Fraser & Dunlop; 'Van Gogh's Yellow Chair' by Mark Roper reprinted by permission of Dedalus Press, image by permission of the National Gallery of Ireland; 'Tich Miller' by Wendy Cope from *Making Cocoa for Kingsley Amis,* reproduced by permission of Faber and Faber; The Irish Cancer Society; Nokia; BMW; Nike; *The Irish Daily Star; The Irish Times; RTE Guide; Teen Vogue Magazine; Garden Magazine; Justine Magazine; Shoot Magazine; Q Magazine; RTE; Newstalk; TG4; BBC; UTV; RTE Stills Library;* Aongus Collins/*Sunday Tribune,* Anglo-Irish Bank cartoon, reproduced by permission; Piece of Paper cartoon, reproduced by permission of the *Irish Independent;* Aliens Viewing Plant Earth reproduced by permission of Martyn Turner; *Pompeii* book cover, © Random House Inc, from *Pompeii* by Robert Harris, used by permission of Random House Inc; US National Oceanic and Atmospheric Administration; 'The Taming of the Shrew' image courtesy of The Ark Theatre Company, Los Angeles, CA, USA.

While considerable effort has been made to locate all holders of copyright material used in this book we have been unsuccessful in contacting some. Should they wish to contact Educate.ie we will be happy to come to an arrangement.

All trademarks reproduced or mentioned in this publication are the property of their respective owners.

Other images courtesy of BigStock, Stockbyte/Getty, Vector Stock.